From Rejected to Redeemed

Overcoming the Plan of the Enemy

Tuwana Nicole

From Rejected to Redeemed

From Rejected to Redeemed: Overcoming the Plan of the Enemy.

Copyright @ 2019 by Better Than Blessed Enterprises, All Rights Reserved.

Printed in the United States of America

The Library of Congress Cataloging-in-Publication Data:

Application for cataloging has been submitted at the time of print.

ISBN-13: 9781686632075

Unless otherwise stated, Scripture is taken from *The NIV/Message Parallel Study Bible (NIV) (MSG)*

All quotes by others have been given credit within actual quotes.

Definitions taken from Wikipedia

Book cover designed by Pasindu Lakshan

Photos by Gregory Lopez Photography

Book Interior Design, Format, and Publishing by

Tuwana Nicole

Table of Contents

From Rejected to Redeemed

Acknowledgement

Dear Heavenly Father,

My Creator, my Savior, my Lord, my Husband, my Comforter, my Protector, my Provider, and my Best Friend; words cannot express my gratitude for who you are to me. I never thought I could be completely free. But you O' Lord have shown me that anything is possible when I keep my focus on you.

You have shown me how to love like you because you are love. You've shown me how to break the cycle of dysfunction and to live a redeemed life that is only found in a relationship with you. You have exceeded my wildest dreams in every area of my life.

I am so thankful for your pursuit of me because you knew the deepest longings of my heart and you knew that only you could ever satisfy them. I am so thankful for your grace and mercy keeping me when I did not understand what your purpose was for my life.

I thank you for entrusting me again to become the answer to my prayers so that others will have an example to follow. I pray that the insight and revelation that I give in this book will bring transformation in the lives of all who read it. I pray that everyone who reads this book will go from rejected to redeemed and overcome the plan of the enemy.

In the Mighty Name of Jesus I pray,

Amen!

Dedication

This book is dedicated to my children Kashun and Kennedy. Though you may not completely understand the journey that God has me on, prayerfully one day you will be able to look back at my life through the lens of the books and ministry that God has entrusted to me and use them as a guide to help both of you develop the courage to follow the voice of God even if no one else understands what you are doing and even if you have to go at it alone. Just know that God is always with you even when people reject you. My prayer is that God's redeeming power will always lead you no matter what's going on around you.

Love Always,

Mom

Introduction

From Rejected

He gives the rejects his hand, and leads them step-by-step.

Psalms 25:9 MSG

I spent so much of my life walking around feeling like a reject because of the way that my life had begun. If you've had the honor of reading my first book "Becoming Comfortable In Your Own Skin" or attending the Becoming Comfortable In Your Own Skin Workshop, you know how being the product of an adulterous relationship, molestation, and abuse; led to me having feelings of rejection that led me down a path that was destined for destruction.

I did not know that everything that I was experiencing was because of a real unseen enemy that had no intentions of stopping until he ultimately destroyed me and thwarted God's purpose for my life. This enemy is always looking for any and every opportunity that we give to him. He knows that if he has any opportunity, he can eventually take over.

Unknown to the enemy or myself, God had another plan all along. It took me a long time to understand God's plan, but I know that being rejected was merely a redirection for God to get the glory out of life.

If you have been feeling rejected, abandoned, overwhelmed, crazy, unloveable, like a failure, or suicidal; know that God wants to get the glory out of your life too! As you follow my story From Rejected to Redeemed, I pray that you will begin to see that EVERYTHING you have ever wanted and needed will be provided by God.

I pray that your mind battles will go away, your money problems will go away, your body will be healed from every sickness and disease, your need to be loved by people will go away because you begin to feel the love of your Heavenly Father (the lover of your soul), and you will no longer walk around feeling defeated.

I pray that you will recognize the hand of the enemy in your own personal life and the fire that the enemy set to destroy you will ignite a fire within you to align your will with the will of your Heavenly Father so you can overcome the plans of the enemy.

"I'm not saying that I have it all together, that I have it made. But I am well on my way, reaching out for Christ, who has so wondrously reached out for me. Friends, don't get me wrong; by no means do I count myself an expert in all of this, but I've got my eye on the goal, where God is beckoning us onward- to Jesus. I'm off and running and I'm not turning back."

Philippians 3:12-14 MSG

"I have been made a messenger of this wonderful news by the gift of grace that works through me. Even though I am the least significant of all his holy believers, this grace-gift was imparted when the manifestation of his power came upon me. Grace alone empowers me so that I can boldly preach this wonderful message to non-Jewish people, sharing with them the unfading, inexhaustible riches of Christ, which are beyond comprehension. My passion is to enlighten every person to this divine mystery. It was hidden for ages past until now, and kept a secret in the heart of God, the Creator of all. The purpose of this was to unveil before every throne and rank of angelic orders in the heavenly realm God's full and diverse wisdom revealed through the church. This perfectly wise plan was destined from eternal ages and fulfilled completely in our Lord Jesus Christ, so that now we have boldness through him, and free access as kings before the Father because of our complete confidence in Christ's faithfulness."

Ephesians 3:7-12 TPT

Before we begin this journey from Rejected to Redeemed. I wanted to take this time to define a few words that I will be using interchangeably throughout the book.

God has appeared to me the following ways:

God, the Father

God, the Son

God, the Holy Spirit

These are the ways that I will refer to HIM throughout the book based on the different ways that I have experienced HIS presence. I always distinguish God with either a capital first letter or all caps.

God, Jesus, Creator, my everything, Holy Spirit, Heavenly Father, Daddy, Jesus Christ, Christ, Life light, Lord, and Savior

Genesis 1:26

I will refer to the devil as the enemy or the serpent. I will also refer to him in other ways, but will notate at the beginning of the chapters.

Part 1

Who Is the Real Enemy?

Enemy is translated from the Hebrew word literally meaning "one who hates". Some synonyms are adversary, foe, accuser, deceiver, devil, demon, serpent, dragon, or rival.

So the great dragon was thrown down once and for all. He was the serpent, the ancient snake called the devil, and Satan, who deceives the whole earth. He was cast down into the earth and his angels along with him.

Revelation 12:9 TPT

Chapter 1

Satan is god

Satan, who is the god of this world has blinded the minds of those who don't believe. They are unable to see the glorious light of the Good News. They don't understand this message about the glory of Christ, who is the exact likeness of God.

2 Corinthians 4:4 TPT

You may be saying to yourself, why is Tuwana taking the time to tell me who Satan is when I already know who he is, right? I dare to say that many people think they know who Satan is. If someone had made the same statement to me about fifteen years ago, I may have thought the same thing.

However, after struggling for many years in my walk with God; I couldn't understand why there always seemed to be some type of opposition against me. I knew God loved me and I loved Him, but I could never seem to be free from some of my past issues.

After looking back over my life, my family history, and deepening my relationship with God; I came to the realization that I only saw Satan as a former angel who was condemned to spend eternity in hell (2 Peter 2:4 NLT). I never really thought about the impact he was having on my life, those around me, and the world over. Satan is a fallen angel that was cast out of heaven because he was very prideful and wanted to be God. Since he was cast out of heaven, he has made it a priority to hinder God's plan for mankind.

2 Corinthians 4:4 TPT describes Satan as the god of this world. I had read that scripture many times over the years, but it never really dawned on me that the world that I live in is the actual "world" that Satan rules. Quite honestly, I was always perplexed by the things that were happening in the world. I would always say things like, "what in the world is going on?"; "why in the world would anyone do that?; or "what is this world coming to?' I couldn't understand why there could be so many evil people in the world.

Satan and his Angels

When Satan was cast down to the earth, he brought other angels with him. Because they chose to follow Satan, he became their leader and now they obey him in the earth. Their goal is to incite rebellion to God among God's created beings (you & me). Scripture doesn't tell us exactly how many angels he has working with him, but we know that they attempt to blind our minds and ultimately possess us so we are unable to see what God wants to do in and through us. Since they are now fallen angels, the Bible refers to them as demons because they have chosen to become messengers of Satan instead of messengers of God. Everywhere you turn all you see is hate. Racism, Sexism, Murder, Deceit, Manipulation, Classism, and Division are just a few of the ways you see the devil at work. The Bible describes Satan in John 8:44 NLT as:

"For you are the children of your father the devil, and you love to do the evil things that he does. He was a murderer from the beginning. He has always hated the truth, because there is no truth in him. When he lies, it is consistent with his character, for he is a liar and the father of lies."

Revelation Moment

Ah ha! Now I'm beginning to understand why the world is so evil! This is the reason why life can be so difficult. This is the reason why generations of my family suffered and struggled. This is the reason why I felt like a reject most of my life. This is the reason MY LIFE had been a mystery for so long!

As I began to digest this truth, I began to grasp exactly who the real enemy is. Where I once was perplexed, I found myself going to God and His inspired Word, The Holy Bible for the answers. As I continued to search, no longer did I have to ask the same questions as before. It became very clear what is happening and exactly what this world is coming to! Satan and anyone who follows his ways is the personification of evil itself!

But the one who indulges in a sinful life is of the devil, because the devil has been sinning from the beginning.

1 John 3:8a TPT

Chapter 2

Why is Satan Allowed to Exist?

Then there was a war in heaven. Michael and his angels were fighting against the dragon and its angels. And the dragon lost the battle, and he and his angels were forced out of heaven. But terror will come on the earth and the seas, for the devil has come down to you in great anger, knowing that he has little time."

Revelation 12:7-8, 12b NLT

After it became clear to me who the real enemy is, I began to ask the question: "Why is Satan allowed to exist?" I was always confused at his ability to control people and make them act a certain way. I could barely decipher if it was Satan working or if it was just in people to act that way. I didn't really understand why God would allow him to continue to exist among his created beings that were made in HIS image!

For in him was created the universe of things, both in the heavenly realm and on the earth, all that is seen and all that is unseen. Every seat of power, realm of government, principality, and authority—it all exists through him and for his purpose!

1 Colossians 1:16 TPT

God began to lead me to examples in the Bible like the life of Job. Then I began to understand that Satan has a purpose. Because Satan is an angel he has power, but he only has the authority that God gives him. God threw Satan down to earth and uses him to test our faith. God wants to see if we want Him more than we want what Satan has to offer in his world!

Revelation Moment

Since Satan is allowed to exist to test our faith. I began to see the parallels with my life and Job's life. In January 2009, when I made the decision to wholeheartedly follow God; my life was pretty amazing! Everything was coming into alignment with God's purpose for my life. I was beginning to see God's hand in my life. I finally felt loved, accepted, and needed. I sensed the presence of Angels protecting me and my household. Miracles were happening on a regular basis.

Revelation 12:12b tells us that Satan will bring terror down to Earth because he is angry for being cast out of heaven. After getting God's permission to test me, the true tests of my faith began. We live in a fallen world because it is controlled by a fallen angel and nothing would please him more than *to "steal, kill, and destroy us."- John 10:10a*

"The Enemy is always taking, God is always giving."

-Tuwana Nicole

Chapter 3

Why We are a Target

For the Enemy

Now that we understand that God created Satan to test our faith, it should be becoming clearer why we are a target for him. Not only is it his job, he is pretty good at it. Satan has been attempting to thwart the plans of God since the beginning in the Garden of Eden.

Target is defined as a person, object, or place selected as the aim of an attack. Satan is a force that comes against our faith. He tries to degrade and minimize our value through repeated attacks to our mind, body, and soul. The enemy is a defeated foe that wants to silence us and keep us bound in the chains of sin.

Since his authority is limited, we are consistently on the enemy's radar. But before the beginning of time, God already had a plan at work to intercept the plan of the enemy.

2 Timothy 1:9 NLT tells us that, *For God saved us and called us to live a holy life. He did this, not because we deserved it, but because that was his plan from before the beginning of time—to show us his grace through Christ Jesus.*

The enemy targets us before we realize that he is already defeated. We spend so much of our lives contending with him when all we have to do is crush him under our feet. Because the devil has picked at us through many generations of our families, many of us don't recognize the power that we have over him. The curse that God put on Him will always be true. We just need to embrace this truth and begin to walk in it and put the enemy under our feet where he belongs!

And I will put enmity (open hostility) Between you and the woman, And between your seed (offspring) and her Seed; He shall [fatally] bruise your head, And you shall [only] bruise His heel.

GENESIS 3:15 AMP

Revelation Moment

1. The Enemy Steals Our Identity
Because we were created in the image of God, the enemy wants to distort our view of God. Satan absolutely hates the fact that we are made in the image of God and he is defeated. He fights to keep us from ever knowing who we are. He keeps baiting us with lies so we remain clueless to his hooks.

2. The Enemy Kills Our Purpose
He hates that we have free will to choose God. He hates that God gives us grace to come back into a right relationship with Him after we have messed up. Most importantly, he hates that there is nothing he can do to win no matter how many of us he tries to deceive. If he can steal our identity, he knows that we will never walk in our purpose.

3. The Enemy Destroys Our Soul
Since Satan has been condemned to eternal damnation and as the old saying goes, "misery loves company." He knows that there is no redemption for him so he wants to take out as many people as he possibly can. If the enemy can get us to deny God, he knows that we will end up just like him. We will spend our lives living for self and ultimately destroy our own souls.

From Rejected to Redeemed

The enemy is always taking, but God is always giving. That's why God gave us himself manifested in human form as Jesus Christ to save us from the plan of the enemy. So even though we are a target for the enemy, we don't have to take the bait, we can simply crush him under our feet!

"The devil is giving you a strategy to kill yourself. Stop taking the bait."

–Tuwana Nicole

Part 2

How the Enemy Operates

Operate means to exert power or influence, to produce an appropriate effect.

Stay alert! Watch out for your great enemy, the devil. He prowls around like a roaring lion, looking for someone to devour.

1 Peter 5:8 NLT

Chapter 4

Temptation to Doubt

Now the serpent was more crafty (subtle, skilled in deceit) than any living creature of the field which the Lord God had made. And the serpent (Satan) said to the woman, "Can it really be that God has said, you shall not eat from any tree of the garden?

Genesis 3:1 AMP

Even though I was beginning to understand who the real enemy is, I didn't quite understand how he operated. Adam and Eve was not aware of his plan when they encountered him in the Garden of Eden. In fact, we can look at Adam and Eve as babies because they were the 1st created beings. Just like a little baby, they walked around naked without knowledge that they were naked. They did not experience childhood, having a mother and father, or friends and family. They had absolutely no examples to follow. They only knew what God had instructed them to do: to tend the garden and...

But the Lord God warned him, "You may freely eat the fruit of every tree in the garden-except the tree of the knowledge of good and evil. If you eat its fruit, **you are sure to die."**-Genesis 2:16 NLT

The enemy is so crafty because he decided that instead of addressing Adam, whom the command was given to directly. He decided to go to Eve, the weaker partner or the younger baby (1 Peter 3:7 NIV). Even though the command was given directly to Adam, we know by her response that Adam did inform her of what God had instructed him to do.

"You won't die!" the serpent replied to the woman. "God knows that your eyes will be opened as soon as you eat it, and you will be like God, knowing both good and evil."-Genesis 3:4 NLT

Adam and Eve allowed the enemy to tempt them to doubt God by saying that they would be like God if they ate the fruit. Even though being like God is the ultimate goal of mankind, we cannot defy God's authority to accomplish it. Because Satan wanted to be God, that's what got him kicked out of heaven in the first place.

The enemy leads us astray by making sin appear to be good by tempting us to doubt God's way and to make us believe that we can be like God by doing what we desire to do without getting God's permission. Satan also makes us believe that God doesn't really care about us and is afraid that we will know more than He does. Satan is so crafty that he will change one Word to attempt to deceive us. God said you will die, Satan says you won't die. Because what Satan is saying sounds good and oftentimes looks good, and we don't understand upfront how one small act of disobedience can shatter our entire lives.

The Shame & Blame Game

*"At that moment their eyes were opened, and they suddenly **felt shame at their nakedness.** So they sewed fig leaves together to cover themselves. When the cool evening breezes were blowing, the man and his wife heard the Lord God walking about in the garden. So they hid from the Lord God among the trees. Then the Lord God called to the man, "Where are you?" He replied, "I heard you walking in the garden, **so I hid. I was afraid because I was naked." "Who told you that you were naked?"** the Lord God asked. "Have you eaten from the tree whose fruit I commanded you not to eat?" **The man replied, "It was the woman you gave me who gave me the fruit, and I ate it."** Then the Lord God*

*asked the woman, "What have you done?" **"The serpent deceived me," she replied. "That's why I ate it."***

Genesis 3:7-13 NLT

Shame is a painful feeling of humiliation or distress caused by the consciousness of wrong behavior. Because they knew they had disobeyed God, they knew they were naked. Their nakedness is synonymous with shame. Just like Adam and Eve, we attempt to cover up our nakedness. We try to cover up and hide our sins from God. Instead of us running to God, we run away from Him. Our running away can lead us to other sins. If we're not careful to repent, we will end up forfeiting God's plan for our lives.

Blame is defined as assigning responsibility for a fault or wrong. Neither Adam nor Eve wanted to take responsibility for their behavior. They placed the blame on each other. Adam blamed Eve and Eve blamed the devil. You see this play out today. Men blame the women and the women blame the men. When are we going to take responsibility for our own relationship with God? When are we going to arise and take our rightful place in the Kingdom? When are going to allow God to grow us up in Him?

Revelation Moment

Because we are the descendants of Adam and Eve, we are all born into a life of sin that can only be redeemed through faith in Jesus, who is the only ONE who lived a sinless life! (2 Corinthians 5:21) The enemy always shows up in our infancy rather it be our physical birth or our spiritual birth. His goal is to get us to give up on God's plan and give in to his plan.

Satan used the same strategy with me that he had used with Adam and Eve. He offered me the temptation to doubt God by making me question everything about God. I questioned if I was even made in the image of God (who I am) because of the way I was conceived. I questioned why God would create me if this is the way my life would be (blamed God). I even questioned why God would allow me to be born into an adulterous relationship (blamed my parents).

Because I took the temptation to doubt, I ended up living much of my life feeling like God would never accept me. I always questioned if I would ever be worthy of His love. Because the enemy convinced me to doubt God, I developed deep feelings of rejection (shame). Because I always felt that God had rejected me, I could never put my trust in God. Ultimately, I began me to trust in myself.

Now it's beginning to become very clear why the enemy came for me when I was born (1975 physical birth) and born again in Christ (1987 and 2009 spiritual births). His goal was to make me give up on God before I could mature enough to understand who God is and what God's plan is for my life.

The temptation to doubt leads to denial of God. Denial of God leads to disobedience to the will of God. Then disobedience separates us from God and keeps us from fulfilling His plan for our lives.

"The devil is just like a boogeyman, he attacks while you're sleeping-stay woke!"

-Tuwana Nicole

Chapter 5

Fear

*I took you from the ends of the earth, from its farthest corners I called you. I said, 'You are my servant', **I have chosen you and have not rejected you. So do not fear**, for I am with you; do not be dismayed, for I am your God. I will strengthen you and help you; I will uphold you with my righteous right hand.*

Isaiah 41:9-10 NIV

What is Fear?

Sin can cause you to feel shame and blame others. If we don't turn from our sin, it can lead us to a life of fear. Fear is defined as a distressing emotion aroused by impending danger, evil, or pain, whether the threat is real or imagined; the feeling or condition of being afraid. Fear is very powerful and can be difficult to control. It can freeze us in place and make it hard for us to protect ourselves. It attacks our ability to trust. It compromises our ability to relax in relationships. It takes over our thought processes, and we have trouble focusing and learning.

Scared Into Silence

From the time I was a very little girl I can remember watching scary (horror) movies with my family. I enjoyed watching them, but would always be very scared to go to bed after watching them. I can remember my older siblings coming by my bedroom making scary noises. I would put my head under my covers and wouldn't dare move or say a word until the next morning.

Even though I was scared, I was always intrigued by scary movies. I spent all of my childhood and the bulk of my adult life watching scary movies. It is something about darkness and evil that seemed to lure me in. No matter how scared I was, I couldn't seem to stop watching with my mouth wide open unable to speak. The enemy used my fear as a tool to scare me into silence about the abuse I had experienced. By being exposed to His ways at such a young age in real life and on TV, I hid my feelings and learned to pretend that I was ok.

How Fear Can Show Up In Our Life

We often repress intense fear. Because we don't want to deal with it, we will simply go to sleep to keep from showing that we're scared. We sleep by pushing it down and masking it with other emotions like anger, depression, and anxiety. If we grow up with fear as a major organizer of our emotional life, we have difficulty developing trusting relationships. When we do connect with people, we have trouble being real. We think we have to wear a mask of whatever that we think that will make us accepted by that person or group. So we will pretend to be something that we're not, then that causes unnecessary friction and a continual cycle of rejection because we have rejected ourselves. The devil acts just a boogeyman, he paralyzes us into the fear of the unknown.

The Root to Our Fears

Are you afraid of what other people think or say about you? Are you afraid that nobody understands you? Are you afraid of losing friends? Are you ashamed that you don't have it all together? Are you ashamed of the problems that you are experiencing? There was a time when I could answer yes to all of these questions.

From Rejected to Redeemed

The enemy has tried to silence me many times over the years not only through my shame of not having it all together, but through my fear of what people would think about me. Because of my fear of rejection, I still had a desire to control my life.

My fear of rejection continued to show up in the form of anger, temper tantrums, and depression because deep down I feared I would always be rejected. I just wanted to be accepted and loved. I would have periods of contentment, but that desire would always be lurking in the background. It wasn't until I faced the test of loyalty to self or God that I finally overcame my fears.

How then does a man gain the essence of wisdom? We cross the threshold of true knowledge when we live in obedient devotion to God. Stubborn know-it-alls will never stop to do this, for they scorn true wisdom and knowledge.

Proverbs 1:7 TPT

By never receiving the type of love that I needed as a child, the enemy toyed with me all of my childhood and most of my adult life by making me believe that I didn't need anyone, including God. In my attempts to control my life, I actually did more harm than good in my attempts.

I still struggled with trusting people. I hurt myself and continually allowed myself to be further damaged by allowing people that were sent by the enemy to deceive, manipulate, use, abuse, and ultimately reject me.

Just like a little child, I was unable to address my fear so I would try to go to sleep (put on my mask, get a drink, have sex, work harder, escape through travel, get into a new relationship, or anything just to ease my mind and to be able to cope with my life) hoping that when I woke up (when I get to heaven in the presence of God), the boogeyman would be gone. But he continued to show back up the next night and the next night until I decided to actually wake up (surrender to God) and deal with issues in my heart.

There is no fear in love. But perfect love drives out fear, because fear has to do with punishment. The one who fears is not made perfect in love. We love because he first loved us.

John 4:18-19 NIV

Stop Sleeping on God

Even though I knew that God is love. I could never put my faith in God as the source of love because I believed the lies of Satan that I could do it on my own. He is just like a boogeyman; he showed up while I was sleeping on God and scared me into believing I couldn't depend on anyone, but myself.

Keep a cool head. Stay alert. The devil is poised to pounce, and would like nothing better than to catch you napping.

1 Peter 5:8 MSG

I thought I could handle being rejected by seeking solace the things of this world. So I wasted a lot of time seeking out love in people (lust of the flesh), places (lust of the eyes), and things (pride of life).I began to realize that I hadn't fully received God's (Our Creator & Heavenly Father) love for me because I was still sleeping. Because I was still operating from a place of rejection, I couldn't trust in Him to lead, guide, protect, and deliver me from myself and my desires to control my life.

Take off the Mask

And no wonder, since Satan himself masquerades as an angel of light. So it is no great surprise if his servants also masquerade as servants of righteousness, but their end will correspond with their deeds.

2 Corinthians 11:14-15 AMP

I got so used to the storms of life that I began to conform by wearing masks so my fear wouldn't show. I thought if I just fit in with the crowd, no one would notice that I was pretending to have it all together. I was pretending to be happy. A mask simply hides the real you.

I had been wearing several masks:

Mask of Intelligence-You are smart and excel in school or anything you attempt to do. You may have been the first one to graduate in your family, received scholarships and grants.

For it is written: "I will destroy the wisdom of the wise; the intelligence of the intelligent I will frustrate.

1 Corinthians 1:19 NIV

Mask of Success-You may have a great career, be a good friend, or be a good parent. You have come out of poverty. You are able to give your children what your parents weren't able to give you.

Though they have the greatest rewards of this world and all applaud them for their accomplishments, they will follow those who have gone before them and go straight into the realm of darkness, where they never ever see the light again. So this is the way of mortal man— honored for a moment, yet without eternal insight, like a beast that will one day perish.

Psalms 49:18-20 TPT

Mask of Relationship Status-You may feel like your life is complete now that you are married or have a significant other. You're elated that someone loves you.

Jesus said, "Marriage is a major preoccupation here, but not there. Those who are included in the resurrection of the dead will no longer be concerned with marriage nor, of course, with death.

Luke 20:34-35 MSG

Mask of Religion-You go to church, but do not have an intimate relationship with God.

Anyone who sets himself up as "religious" by talking a good game is self-deceived. This kind of religion is hot air and only hot air. Real religion, the kind that passes muster before God the Father, is this: Reach out to the homeless and loveless in their plight, and guard against corruption from the godless world.

James 1:26-27 MSG

Mask of Independence-You don't need nobody. You are the superhero of your own life. You don't even need God. You think you are free, but you are actually becoming the god of your own life just like Satan, our Enemy.

You are busy analyzing the Scriptures, frantically poring over them in hopes of gaining eternal life. Everything you read points to me, yet you still refuse to come to me so I can give you the life you're looking for—eternal life! "I do not accept the honor that comes from men, for I know what kind of people you really are, and I can see that the love of God has found no home in you. I have come to represent my Father, yet you refuse to embrace me in faith. But when someone comes in their own name and with their own agenda, you readily accept him. Of course you're unable to believe in me. For you live for the praises of others and not for the praise that comes from the only true God.

John 5:39-44 TPT

Revelation Moment

Since we are fearful of sitting in our truth, we allow the enemy to scare us into silence. Because he has been haunting us our entire lives, he wants us to believe he is simply a boogeyman. No one believes that a boogeyman is real. Then we end up spending our lives becoming exactly who he wants us to be . We end up becoming just like him because are pretending to be happy, but we've never gotten past the age when we realized that not telling the truth is not ok. So we go through life pretending that everything is ok when in essence all we're doing is accumulating masks that only further dilute our minds and keep us from being who we really are.

I achieved success in school and in my career. But, I was still struggling because of my inability to get the love that I was so desperately searching for. My inability to control the outcome of my life led me to a dark place. I continued in this cycle for many years until I became suicidal. Because I wasn't allowing God to renew my mind, I was becoming my own god. It was easy to put on all the different masks because I had been doing it almost my entire life. I had to "fake it until I make it"!

The Enemy wants us to always be torn between what this world has to offer and what God is offering us. If he keeps us scared long enough, he ends up silencing us through our fears.. If he can't silence us through our fears, he will silence us by luring us to become the god of our own lives by wearing the mask of independence. All of the attacks are to ultimately demonize (possess) us.

When I began to allow Jesus' redemptive work to sink in, I was able to be honest about where I was. I no longer felt the need to put on a mask to hide my fears any longer. I was able to take off all the masks I had been wearing and be naked before God. I began to learn how to face my issues head on as I continued to allow my Heavenly Father to work in my life, knowing I can continue to overcome my fears as long remain obedient to Him.

For we are not given a spirit of fear, but of power, love, and self-discipline.

2 Timothy 1:7 NLT

I began learning more about God's perfect love and learning not be anxious about anything, but in everything, by prayer and petition, with thanksgiving, present my requests to my Heavenly Father (Philippians 4:6-7). I began to talk to him about everything, even the things that I was ashamed to share with anyone else.

I believed that God loved me and I thank him for His love. Now I am walking in peace, not fear. I constantly remind myself that this is a daily decision to give all my cares and fears to my Heavenly Father and commit to trusting in His love.

Your Heavenly Father loves you too and doesn't want you to be held captive by fear and its' byproducts any longer. If you take off the masks, you will no longer be blinded from the truth. You will begin to see that EVERYTHING you needed, will be provided by God. You will no longer walk around in fear of anything, including the devil!

Pray this simple prayer to help you continually give all your cares to God:

Dear Heavenly Father,

Thank you for loving me. Thank you for giving me a spirit of power, love, and self-discipline. Help me to trust you more and to accept your perfect love. I know that only then can I overcome fear.

In the Mighty Name of Jesus,

Amen.

"Don't be so paralyzed by fear that you lose your power, your mind, and your ability to love!"-

Tuwana Nicole

Chapter 6

Attacks The Mind

If our minds are ruled by our desires, we will die. But if our minds are ruled by the Spirit, we will have life and peace.

Romans 8:6 CEVUK

In September 2008, I found myself in the psychiatric ward at St. Francis Hospital. I had been contemplating murdering my children and committing suicide. Life had become too hard me to bear any longer. I had been told I was crazy so many times growing up that I began to believe it. I had tried everything I could think of. I had tried over 20 different antidepressants since I was in my mid 20's.

As good as I had tried to be, my entire life was leading me straight to the pit of hell (Proverbs 12:28). With my long list of heartache and pain, there was nothing to live for. I was at the end of my rope hanging on to the threads of my raggedy life. I looked over my life. This is all I could see:

- ❖ Bastard child
- ❖ Molested
- ❖ Abused
- ❖ Rejected
- ❖ Abandoned
- ❖ I tried to think positive
- ❖ I tried to live for God
- ❖ I tried to Love myself
- ❖ I tried to Love others
- ❖ I tried EVERYTHING!

I can't take it anymore. I realized that I could not do it in my own strength. This can't be what life is all about. If God really loved me, why would He allow me to go through this nightmare that I couldn't seem to wake up from!

My Mother was a Believer

Just six months prior to me getting to the end of my rope, my Mother was brutally murdered by the husband of a woman she was helping. The woman had come to my Mother's church needing help because her husband was on drugs. My Mother took up with the woman and her son, helping them during their time of need even allowing them to come to her home. My Mother was truly being the hands and feet of Jesus for this family.

Over the course of time, the woman decided to take her drug addicted husband back. She introduced him to my Mother and even brought him to my Mother's home. After spending a little time together, they left. The husband comes back to my Mother's house the next day. Because she has already met him, she invited him in and offered him a cup of coffee.

He proceeds to ask my Mother for $20. My Mother tells him no, then she goes to the kitchen to get the coffee. As she turns her back, he hits her in the back of the head with a hammer. After murdering her, he proceeds to steal any valuables he could find in her home as well as her purse.

My brother finds her body the next morning when he goes to pick her up for church. The police trace my Mother's credit cards and are able to track him down within 24 hours. He pleads guilty and is given a life sentence. The details of the murder were in his confession.

From Rejected to Redeemed

Though he was given a life sentence, the enemy riddled me with guilt by saying things like, "what kind of daughter are you?" and "If you had been there, you could've stopped this from happening." I was supposed to be at her house that weekend, but I changed my mind at the last minute because I wanted to go to the casino to mask the pain of my miserable life. I was severely depressed, overweight, and gambling to mask the pain. I chose to go to the casino that weekend instead of going to visit my Mother.

I was so angry at God for allowing this to happen to my Mother. She was a woman of faith. She wasn't perfect, but I had seen her growth and her desire to know God more. She was a prayer warrior so I'm like WHY GOD? Why would you allow someone who is living for you to die like this?

I would soon realize that I had been asking the right questions. In fact, I had been asking the right questions my entire life. My only problem is that I was listening to the wrong one!

*I'm hurting Lord-will you forget me forever? How much longer, Lord? Will you look the other way when I'm in need? How much longer must I cling to this constant grief? I've endured this **shaking of my soul**. So how much longer will my enemy have the upper hand? It's been long enough!*

Psalms 13:1-2 TPT

I had been asking God, but I would always listen to what the enemy instead of God. I struggled to discern God's voice from the voice of the enemy/inner me. I had come from a long line of generational curses that had been passed down in my blood line due to rebellion. Because my ancestors (Isaiah 43:27) had conformed to the way of the world, it left my family open to demonization. No matter how much I wanted to be good and do good; I would only be able to break the curses through surrender to God.

"And do not be conformed to this world [any longer with its superficial values and customs], but be transformed and progressively changed [as you mature spiritually] by the renewing of your mind [focusing on godly values and ethical attitudes], so that you may prove [for yourselves] what the will of God is, that which is good and acceptable and perfect [in His plan and purpose for you]."

Romans 12:2 AMP

What is Demonization?

Demonization is defined as the possession of the human mind and body by demons. Demons are fallen angels who decided to follow Satan in his rebellion against God. The Bible refers to them as evil spirits under the control of Satan. They help Satan tempt people to sin against God.

One night while lying in my hospital bed in the psychiatric ward, I found myself at the feet of Jesus. Jesus told me that He was who I had been looking for my entire life. He told me that he was the answer to all of the questions that I had asked over the years. He told me that He was the answer to my depression, my desire to be loved (spirit of rejection), my need for validation, EVERYTHING!

Do you see the difference? Sacrifices offered to idols are offered for nothing, for what's the idol but a nothing? Or worse than a nothing, a minus, a demon! I don't want you to become part of something that **reduces you to less than yourself. And you can't have it both ways, banqueting with the Master one day and slumming with demons the next.** *Besides, the Master won't put up with it. He wants us-all or nothing. Do you think you can get off with anything less?*

1 Corinthians 10:19-22 MSG

One generation's compromise is the next generation's standard. I didn't have to go back more than one generation in my family history to see that plan of the enemy was working overtime. Our subtle disobedience over time had distanced our family from God.

They will act religious, but they will reject the power that can make them godly. They are always learning but never discover the revelation-knowledge of truth.

2 Timothy 3:5a, 7 NLT & TPT

Though I came from a family who went to church, we had denied its' power to completely transform our lives more into the image of Christ over the years. So instead, the door was left open for the enemy to infiltrate the family legacy and to pervert what my ancestors had originally purposed for us.

Mental Illness is the

Portal for Demonization

Mental illness also called mental health disorders refers to a wide range of mental health conditions that affect your mood, thinking, and behavior. Examples include depression, anxiety, schizophrenia, dementia, eating disorders, and addictive behaviors.

Mark 1:23-26 NLT states clearly that you can be religious and attend church, but be demonically possessed.

*Suddenly, a man in the synagogue who was possessed by an evil spirit cried out, "Why are you interfering with us, Jesus of Nazareth? Have you come to destroy us? I know who you are—the Holy One of God!" But Jesus reprimanded him. "Be quiet! Come out of the man," he ordered. At that, **the evil spirit screamed, threw the man into a convulsion,** and then came out of him."*

I had a decision to make. Was I going to continue with life as it has always been and simply accept that I had a mental illness or was I going to believe that this encounter with Jesus was real? Jesus had told me that He was the answer to EVERYTHING? Right? Right! All I needed to do was change my mind so I receive!?

The Master Deceiver

For you are the children of your father the devil, and you love to do the evil things that he does. He was a murderer from the beginning. He has always hated the truth, because there is no truth in him. When he lies, it is consistent with his character, for he is a liar and the father of lies.

John 8:44 NLT

I had spent the bulk of my life being called crazy by people around me, which I now understand that they were being used by Satan to ultimately demonize me. Both me and those he used to deceive me, we're like two peas in a pod headed toward self-destruction under the control of the Enemy.

Do you remember when you were little, your parents would spank you if you told them that they were lying. You may have been told, "what happens in this house stays in this house." You may have been told that no matter what, you never turn on your family, even if it was the same family that abused you, molested you, or fondled you. So then you grow up with an identity crisis. Then the same people who abused you have the nerve to begin calling you crazy, which leads to you believing those lies too. The cycle continues because they are still bound by the enemy.

When we grow up in an environment that tells us that the truth is actually a lie, we get confused. We begin to think something is wrong with us when in fact there is something wrong with the world. Because I wanted to be loved so badly, the enemy used my fear of rejection to make me compromise my truth by accepting anything just so I wouldn't feel rejected. So I stayed in harmful situations too long, did things that I had no business doing, put up with disrespect, abuse, manipulation, cheating, just so I could say that I had a family, friends, and a man!

Now that I understand that this world is run by the devil, it became very clear that he has blinded the eyes of man into believing that demonization is merely a health issue so he could continue to build his kingdom and thwart God's plan for mankind.

I thought about how my constant anxiety had led to my chronic depression. Then how my chronic depression led me to suicidal thoughts. As I looked back over my family history of suicide, attempted suicide, depression, anxiety, bi-polar disorder, dementia, and eating disorders; I knew that I had to make a different choice if I didn't want the curse to continue. My history with the enemy had always led me to constant heartache and pain. And now, he led me to the brink of suicide! Well no more! The devil is a liar!

Revelation Moment

Then I began to look at my history with God. I began to think about the promises he tells us that are in store for those who believe in Him. I knew that God created me. As I began to think about the promises God had made to me when I accepted him at age 13 and now again at age 33; it became overwhelmingly obvious that I had never completely trusted God.

The enemy had offered me the temptation to doubt God again, but I realized what he was offering only led me to denying God. By choosing to remain in a continuous cycle of disobedience to God, I was under his control. This time, Satan was about to destroy me.

From Rejected to Redeemed

In that moment, I didn't know how God was going to be my answer to EVERYTHING. But I came to the realization that I had allowed the enemy to wreck my life for too long. I chose to believe that my encounter with God this time was really real.

Think about this. Wrap your minds around it. This is serious business, rebels. Take it to heart. **Remember your history, I am God, the only God you've had or ever will have-incomparable, irreplaceable-From the very beginning telling you what the ending will be, all along letting you in on what is going to happen.** *Assuring you, "I'm in this for the long haul, I'll do exactly what I set out to do, calling that eagle, Tuwana*, out of the east, from a far country the man (woman) I chose to help me. I've said it and I'll certainly do it. I've planned it, so it's as good as done.*

Isaiah 46:8-11 MSG
*cross out my name and write in your name

Up to this point in life, no one had ever made me feel like this. The last time I had felt this way was when I was 13. This was when I was baptized. Even though I wasn't demonically possessed, those demons had been riding my back my entire life in an attempt to completely over take me. I was gradually being possessed as I my mental health went into decline over the years.

By making the decision to believe the voice of God over my past; what the enemy meant for harm, God was turning it around for my good! I finally felt a sense of freedom that I had never felt before. I finally felt loved, needed, accepted, and appreciated. I had been redeemed!

Now it was beginning to make sense why God had been leading me to books on breaking the cycle of dysfunction in my family and looking for love in all the wrong places when I was 13. God was training me how to break the generational curses in my family! God was showing me His plan for my life!

"You're not asking for too much, you're asking the wrong one. Ask the right ONE. Ask God!"

−Tuwana Nicole

Chapter 7

Distractions

Keep your eyes straight ahead; ignore all sideshow distractions.

Proverbs 4:25 MSG

A distraction is defined as anything that prevents you from giving full attention to something else. As I was beginning to write this chapter, I was distracted by a phone call. I completely lost my train of thought. The enemy wouldn't be doing his job effectively if he wasn't always bringing things to distract us from God's purpose for our lives.

Most things that the enemy sends to distract us are good, but we must have balance. I'm reminded of the story of two sisters Martha and Mary, who had invited Jesus into their home as recorded in Luke 10:38-42. Beginning in verse 40 it reads:

But Martha became exasperated by finishing the numerous household chores in preparation for her guests, so she interrupted Jesus and said, "Lord, don't you think it's unfair that my sister left me to do all the work by myself? You should tell her to get up and help me." The Lord answered her, "Martha, my beloved Martha. Why are you upset and troubled, pulled away by all these distractions? Are they really that important? Mary has discovered the one thing most important by choosing to sit at my feet. She is undistracted and I won't take this privilege from her."

From Rejected to Redeemed

I remember a couple years after beginning my walk with God, the Holy Spirit began to convict me about how I was spending my time. He said' "Tuwana you've gotten so busy serving me that you don't spend enough time basking in my presence." I thought I was spending time with God because I was running a homeless shelter full-time, teaching Bible Study, and serving at church. Much of my frustration came from me getting ahead of God, not actively listening, doing things that God didn't ordain, and wanting things to happen in my timing instead of waiting on the Lord.

As I look back on the many mistakes that I made; I began to realize that those mistakes were a direct reflection of the amount of time that I was spending with God. It's almost impossible to get anything worthwhile accomplished for the glory of God without the presence of God. If we are always busy serving God, when will we have time to bask in his presence?

Many of the setbacks and disappointments that I was experiencing were the result of allowing any and everything, especially what I wanted to do to distract me from spending time with God. Since I had not completely surrendered my will to God at this point in my walk, I found myself always complaining to God instead of simply appreciating who He is to me. Because I had not learned to appreciate God, it was easy for the enemy to distract me.

Set your gaze on the path before you. With fixed purpose, looking straight ahead, ignore life's distractions. Watch where you're going! Stick to the path of truth, and the road will be safe and smooth before you. Don't allow yourself to be sidetracked for even a moment or take the detour that leads to darkness.

Proverbs 4:25-27 TPT

Revelation Moment

1. **Get Organized**-Set boundaries and have a daily schedule, making sure you have set aside time to sit at the feet of Jesus. I have been able to operate without stress and anxiety because I make room for God every day.

2. **Don't get too busy for God**-You can never be effective long term for God without the presence of God. I had been allowing busy work to take priority over tasks that God was leading me to do.

3. **Keep God at the Center**-God must be the main focus every day. As I began to get a singular focus on God, I noticed that I had more time and energy to accomplish more because I didn't expend it on things that have no eternal value. Because I was beginning to learn the heart of God, I was able to discern when something was a distraction versus an opportunity for growth in my relationship with God.

> Will you allow God to interrupt your regularly scheduled broadcast programs to host His presence?

"Complaining changes nothing, appreciation changes everything."

–*Tuwana Nicole*

Chapter 8

Religion: The Great Divider

Let there be no divisions in the church. Rather, be of one mind, united in thought and purpose.

1 Corinthians 1:10b NLT

We see throughout history how religion has divided God's people. The church was intended to be a place of refuge and empowerment for the body of Christ, but we see the enemy hard at work keeping up confusion. God is not the author of confusion, but the enemy is. Remember he was kicked out of heaven for wanting to be God. The battle that eventually had him thrown to earth continues here on earth. Because his goal is to keep us from doing God's Will and fulfilling our purpose here on Earth; he always starts with the body of Christ.

Because the kingdom of the Enemy is so organized; when he comes against your church, your family, your business, and your household; he is coming loaded with ammunition. His demons have a singular focus; to steal, kill and destroy. The unified strategic attack of the enemy is to use the temptation to doubt that leads to confusion and then division.

Who Are You Following?

Many people come to Jesus through a particular person or a group of believers. This is obviously a good thing, however we must be careful that we're not following the person or the group above the Word of God. More importantly the person or group of believers that convert a person needs to be sure that they do not turn the person into a follower of them, but instead turn them into a follower of HIM!

The HIM, I'm referring to is Jesus Christ. In the early church, many were being divided over trivial issues such as who baptized them and following traditions. In today's society many people do the same thing by making a big deal about being a member of a certain group of believers, nationality, skin color, or sex. We have a tendency to disqualify those that are not from the same background as we are.

We must be one in Christ Jesus no matter what nationality we are or what our background is or what group we are a part of. Are you a follower of Jesus or a follower of the church you attend? Are you a follower of Jesus or your women's group? Are you a follower of Jesus or your people?

And we no longer see each other in our former state-Jew or non-Jew, rich or poor, male or female-because we're all one through our union with Jesus Christ with no distinction between us.

Galatians 3:28 TPT

There Will Be Some Division

The only thing that should divide the body of Christ is our loyalty to Jesus, self, and Satan. *Paul states in 1 Corinthians 11:18-19; I've been told many times that when you meet as a congregation, divisions and cliques emerge-and to some extent, this doesn't surprise me. Differences of opinion are unavoidable, yet they will reveal which ones among you truly have God's approval.*

We must be careful not to show partiality toward different believers who don't look like us, talk like us, or even dress like us. When we put our own personal

preferences over the scriptures, we give an opportunity for the enemy to come in. We are not always going to agree on what we would like, but we should always agree on the Word of God.
Now being that we are seeking God's approval, the only thing that should actually divide us is who is living for God and who is not. Our loyalty will dictate our behavior.

*And you know that Jesus came to take away our sins, and there is no sin in him. **Anyone who continues to live in him will not sin.** But anyone who keeps on sinning does not know him or understand who he is. Dear children, don't let anyone deceive you about this: When people do what is right, it shows that they are righteous, even as Christ is righteous. But **when people keep on sinning, it shows that they belong to the devil, who has been sinning since the beginning.** But the Son of God came to destroy the works of the devil. Those who have been born into God's family **do not make a practice of sinning, because God's life is in them.** So they can't keep on sinning, because they are children of God. So now we can tell who are children of God and who are children of the devil. **Anyone who does not live righteously and does not love other believers does not belong to God.***

1 John 3:5-10 NLT

Religion vs. Relationship

After being in church for many years, I came to realize that Satan loves to keep us divided over trivial issues that erode the fabric of Christianity. It seems that more churches and more churches have begun to be more concerned about what religion/denomination is right versus WHO is right, which can lead to pride.

From Rejected to Redeemed

The Kingdom of God is within us. When we make the decision to make Jesus our Lord and our Savior, He sends His Holy Spirit to come to live inside of us. God wants an intimate relationship with us, that's why He patterned the church after marriage (Ephesians 5:23-32).

"The Kingdom of God is within you."
Luke 17:21b NIV

Religion/Denominationalism is man's feeble attempts to obey God by following certain rules that they believe will lead to God. When I think of the word denomination, I always think of the word fraction. A fraction is defined as a small or tiny part of something. So in essence any denomination only has a tiny part of what God intends for His people, but is missing the bigger picture. Most denominations will try to make you think that it is inside of a building or in a certain city, or even represented by a particular group of people. All God wants us to do is:

Come to Me, all who are weary and heavily burdened [by religious rituals that provide no peace], and I will give you rest [refreshing your souls with salvation]. Take My yoke upon you and learn from Me [following Me as My disciple], for I am gentle and humble in heart, and YOU WILL FIND REST (renewal, blessed quiet) FOR YOUR SOULS. For My yoke is easy [to bear] and My burden is light.

MATTHEW 11:28-30 AMP

Instead of the church coming together to rest in God, we allow the enemy to use our differences to divide us. If we understood that on our best day we can't defeat the enemy in our own strength, we would use our commonalities to draw us closer to one another so we can become an unstoppable force. The division that the Enemy causes in our lives leads us to the mask of religion and the mask of independence. We become overloaded with trying to meet all the demands of religion that we never simply surrender to and rest in God. By never truly taking on Jesus' yoke, we remain bound to sin and get weary in our pursuit of Him. Wearing the heavy yoke of religion/denominationalism opens the door to demonization.

One Body, Many Parts

Now these are the gifts Christ gave to the church: the apostles, the prophets, the evangelists, and the pastors and teachers. Their responsibility is to equip God's people to do his work and build up the church, the body of Christ. This will continue until we all come to such unity in our faith and knowledge of God's Son that we will be mature in the Lord, measuring up to the full and complete standard of Christ. Then we will no longer be immature like children. We won't be tossed and blown about by every wind of new teaching. We will not be influenced when people try to trick us with lies so clever they sound like the truth. Instead, we will speak the truth in love, growing in every way more and more like Christ, who is the head of his body, the church. He makes the whole body fit together perfectly. As each part does its own special work, it helps the other parts grow, so that the whole body is healthy and growing and full of love.

Ephesians 4:11-16 NLT

Brief definitions of some of the different parts & gifts of the body of Christ. Each part may have 1 or more gifting:

❖ **Apostle**-brings all the parts together and sets order in the Church. May have many gifts such as prophecy, miracle working, and healing.

- ❖ **Prophet**-serves as the eyes of the church and receives special revelation or instruction from God. May be able to foretell God's future plans.
- ❖ **Evangelist**-spreads the Good News of salvation.
- ❖ **Pastor**-shepherds and guides the local body of Christ.
- ❖ **Teacher**-instructs the Church in the Word of God.
- ❖ **Miracle Worker**-do things that are out of the ordinary or cannot be explained in the natural.
- ❖ **Healer**-heal all forms of sickness and disease by the laying on of hands, praying or speaking over someone.
- ❖ **Speak in different languages**-the ability to speak in different languages so that those who speak in those languages can understand.
- ❖ **Interpretation of different languages**-ability to interpret what someone who is speaking in an unknown language is saying in their native language.

The enemy will use the parts and gifts that God gives us to be a blessing to the body of Christ to divide us from each other and many will fall away because of self-promotion and manipulation of the gifts. We believe that we can function as the body of Christ without all of the parts working together, but this is a plot of the enemy to keep us divided and ultimately conquer and demonize us.

Now you [collectively] are Christ's body, and individually [you are] members of it [each with his own special purpose and function].

1 Corinthians 12:27 AMP

The enemy will continue to keep up separated by strife, jealousy, and pride. So ultimately we become ineffective for the Kingdom of God when God meant for us to work together in unity.

Denominationalism is a

Portal to Demonization

Your hand-to-hand combat is not with human beings, but with the highest principalities and authorities operating in rebellion under the heavenly realms. For they are a powerful class of demon-gods and evil spirits that hold this dark world in bondage.

Ephesians 6:12 TPT

Because the enemy uses subtle divisive ways to possess us, oftentimes it is not noticeable that he is at work even in our pursuit of getting to know God. The enemy tempts us to doubt God. If that doesn't work, he will attack our minds. If cannot get our mind, then he will get us puffed with pride, thinking we know God better than the next believer or that our part or gift is more important so the enemy will use our pride to divide us.

The enemy pits us against each other where we think it's the person, while all along it's the enemy causing problems in the background. Because we can see the person that the enemy is using, we harbor ill will, bitterness, and resentment towards that person not realizing that the enemy is working through them to wreak havoc in the church.

Then many will stop following me and fall away, and they will betray one another and hate one another.

Matthew 24:10 TPT

Next jealousy ensues, then these divisions cause us to go off on our own and do our own thing. This is the reason there are so many denominations today. Everybody doing their own thing and competing with one another instead of coming together for the good of everyone.

Instead of recognizing our need to be more Christ-like by praying for and forgiving one another, we end up either falling away or we have a continuous stream of new denominations forming that take us further away from God's purpose for our lives.

After the enemy has successfully divided us, demonization is imminent because an un-renewed mindset opens up the door for the antichrist to arise through the false prophet. We must make sure we are testing the spirit by the Word of God (1 John 4:1-3). Because we are all separated parts of the body of Christ operating as if we are whole, we don't realize that we need each other to function the way God intended His Church to function.

Unity is Key

I urge you to live a life worthy of the calling you have received. Be completely humble and gentle; be patient bearing with one another in love. Make every effort to keep the unity of the Spirit through the bond of peace. There is one body and one Spirit-just as you were called to one hope when you were called-one Lord, one faith, one baptism, one God and Father of all, who is over all and through all and in all.

Ephesians 4:1-6 NIV

Unity is the state of being united or joined as a whole. As long as the enemy can keep us divided, we will never come into the fullness of who God intends for us to be. Unity is where our growth lies. Unity is where we become a healthy army prepared to withstand the attacks of the enemy.

Our unity in Christ does not destroy our individuality. In fact, our different parts & gifts only enhance the work of Christ in our lives and the world over. As we spiritually mature, we understand the need for all of the parts & gifts of the body of Christ to work together in unity. God gives different parts & gifts as He sees fit (1 Corinthians 12:4-11). So if we reject the parts that we don't like or understand, we are in essence rejecting God.

The enemy understands that we are creatures of habit. He wants us to get comfortable, get a routine, and get religious. He knows that when we get a routine, we are predictable. Our routine is the different religious denominations that we choose to be a part of. He knows when we're sleeping. He knows when we're weak and vulnerable. He knows exactly when to attack and how to attack. He wants to keep surprise attacking us.

The only way we can counter his attacks is to allow God to show us the way. God will have us doing things spontaneously to keep the enemy confused. Only when all of the gifts are working in unity can this happen. Just when the enemy is about to pounce, God's way will pull us to safety. Just when he thought he had us, our obedience to God will have the enemy scratching his head and wondering what happened. By making the decision to do things God's way, we will have the enemy on the run. Instead of our soul shaking, we'll have the enemy shaking for real! (James 2:19)

Revelation Moment

Above all, put on love-the perfect bond of unity.

Colossians 3:14 HCSB

As I began to mature in my faith in God, I realized that many of the questions that I had growing up were simply an overflow of the longing of my soul to see unity in the body of Christ exemplified around me. Even though I was taught about Jesus, I always had lingering questions about why there are so many different churches and how the church that I attended was the only one going to heaven.

Because I was raised in an evangelistic denomination, I always thought that I could only be a teacher and evangelist. I struggled with understanding some of the ways I was different from other people in my church. I was always asking questions, trying to understand why I could see and hear things that others didn't. I can remember having knowledge of things before they happened, but I was told that it was just dejavu (false memory or premonition). No one in my church nor my family knew that God had given me many gifts that were needing to be developed.

I remember God telling me that I would be the generational curse breaker in my family when I was 13. Because of my ignorance and the not being able to receive proper guidance due to division in the church, the enemy tormented my mind for a long time.

As I began to grow in my relationship with God after rededicating myself to Him in 2009, I could see God teaching me in almost every area. I began to have more spiritual clarity as to what God is desiring from those who are following Him. God began to give me dreams and visions that He had given me when I was younger, but now they were beginning to make sense. Now I understand why the enemy wanted me to remain confused about who I am and what God's purpose for my life is. I see why he used many people that should have been loving me to reject me. I see why he wanted me to turn my back on the church completely.

The trivial things that most Christians fight over are merely a plot of the enemy to keep us divided and to keep us from developing and fully maturing into who God intends us to be. By keeping us divided, we can never appreciate the different ways that God (Holy Spirit) works to unify us and help us function as one complete body and ultimately overcome the plan of the enemy as one mighty force of God!

It is time for us to grow up in the body of Christ! It's time out for foolishness. Just because the world is doing it, doesn't mean it's ok for Christians to do it! It has never worked for us, that's why we are called to be a holy and sanctified people! God has given each of us different gifts for us to work together to bring Him glory, not ourselves! The gifts are without repentance, but that doesn't mean that we shouldn't repent. If we keep repentant heart posture, we will see more unity instead of division.

Let's come together in unity and do what God said, like God said to do it! We must be the change in the world that we say we desire to see! It is extremely important for Christians to work together, not against one another. We will never be able to overcome the enemy if we remain divided over worldly issues. Let love be our motivating factor to push forward to living better than blessed!

"Spiritual healing proceeds physical healing. Your faith is the key to your healing."

–*Tuwana Nicole*

Chapter 9

Attacks The Body

"Then the Lord asked Satan, "Have you noticed my servant Job? He is the finest man in all the earth. He is blameless—a man of complete integrity. He fears God and stays away from evil. And he has maintained his integrity, even though you urged me to harm him without cause."
Satan replied to the Lord, "Skin for skin! A man will give up everything he has to save his life. But reach out and take away his health, and he will surely curse you to your face!" "All right, do with him as you please," the Lord said to Satan. "But spare his life." So Satan left the Lord's presence, and he struck Job with terrible boils from head to foot."

Job 2:3-7 NLT

On the night of June 10, 2012; my daughter and I were severely injured during a car accident. While sitting at a red light about 2 minutes prior to the accident, God spoke to me. God clearly said, "Put on your seatbelt." At the time, neither Kennedy or I had on our seatbelts. We were just down the street from our house so I didn't think it was necessary to put on my seatbelt.

I didn't know at the time why God spoke to me, but I simply obeyed. I immediately told Kennedy 3 times to get in her car seat and buckle up. She finally complied about 1 minute prior to us being rear-ended. After we were buckled up, we started singing along with a song that was playing on K-Love. Next thing you know out of nowhere, I felt my body be forcefully jerked in different directions.

We had been hit from the rear and been knocked about 25 feet through the intersection into the turning lane of oncoming traffic. I thank God no other vehicles were coming that could have caused another collision. According to the police report, the driver who hit us had been traveling between 45-50 miles per hour at the point of impact and was ticketed for reckless driving and failure to maintain proper control of her vehicle.

As a result of the collision, our brand new ministry van was totaled. My body was thrown towards the windshield and my seat broke. The only thing that kept me from going through the windshield was the protection of my seatbelt. It seems I blacked out at some point and when I came to, I could hear my daughter crying and I couldn't move my body to help her.

All I can remember is that my head was killing me and my back and neck were hurting. My daughter complained of her neck and legs hurting, not being able to walk. The next thing I knew we were being put in an ambulance and taken to the hospital. We both were diagnosed with a traumatic brain injury (TBI), but they released us from the hospital saying that we would recover within a few days.

Over the course of the next year, my daughter and I struggled with health issues stemming from the car crash. I was diagnosed with severe headaches, retinal detachment, blindness, loss of memory, nerve damage to my spinal cord c5-c7, fibromyalgia, occipital neuralgia, angina, mitral valve prolapse, major depressive disorder, and post-traumatic stress syndrome. I had to close down the homeless shelter that I had run for the past 4 years. I was unable to work due to being in so much pain on a daily basis.

The attacks seemed to come in daily. In one day, I received a diagnosis of hepatitis B and Mono. Then a few weeks later, I received the diagnosis of cirrhosis of the liver. Given the seriousness of this diagnosis, the doctors told me that I would have to be hospitalized if I didn't improve with the new medicine that they were going to prescribe me.

After having a biopsy, it was discovered that there had been many attacks to my liver and the main attack stemmed from my molestation when I was a baby. Because of the severity of the damage, I was given six months to live. While I was awaiting my test results in the waiting room, God asked me, "Whose report are you going to believe, mine or the doctors?" My response was, God, I'm going to believe your report.

It was a struggle to completely trust God in the beginning because I was so accustomed to listening to the doctors over the years. It was also hard because I wanted God to take all of my health issues away at once. At an appointment with one of the ten different specialists that I was seeing, God spoke to me saying, "Didn't I tell you not to go back to this doctor?" God then showed me how He had to allow me to get frustrated with the doctors so I could finally obey His instructions.

God spoke to me again and told me to go back and read the book of Job. He wanted me to understand that everything that was happening to me was to test my faith and see if I would choose His ways over the world's ways. God wanted me to learn how to trust Him in spite of my circumstances.

Revelation Moment

At the time of the accident, I didn't know that God was allowing the enemy to attack my body to test my faith. But, this is the second time that God has audibly spoken to me that I could vividly remember. The funny thing is I had lost a lot of my memory from the car crash, but I began to remember things God had spoken to me when I was younger. I could remember God trying to get my attention in earlier years. It's as if God has written His Word on my heart (Jeremiah 31:33-34). The first time Jesus spoke to me that was undeniable that He was speaking, was when I found myself at His feet while I was in the psychiatric ward. Then again when I'm about to be in a car crash. After my car crash, I began to hear God on a regular basis. Even though He had been speaking all along, it seems that the shouts of world clouded out His voice.

Satan had to get permission from God to attack my body just like he had done with Job. He thought that by attacking my health, I would curse God and die. Even though those were some very dark years where I went back into a deep depression again, I never felt suicidal like I had felt after the murder of my Mother.

God's voice began to get clearer and clearer. He began to give me directions on how to move forward and heal through my experience. By God comparing my situation to Job's situation, I began to develop peace knowing that my troubles wouldn't always last. I knew from reading Job's story that my latter days would be greater than my former days. After reading the book of Job again, it became clear that God allows everything to happen for our good and His glory.

God did exactly what He said He would do. God healed EVERY sickness and disease that plagued my body. He not only healed the issues that stemmed from the car crash, He also restored my vision to 20/20. I had worn glasses since I was five years old. I had always struggled with my weight. God enabled me to lose weight naturally. I had suffered a mild heart attack in my early 20's and had suffered with heart issues from time to time since then. God healed my heart issues. The attacks to my mind that I had struggled with since I was a little girl went away. God reassured me that no plan of the enemy could stop His plan for my life and everything that He has purposed for my life will prevail!

You kissed my heart with forgiveness, in spite of all I've done. You've healed me inside and out from every disease. You've rescued me from hell and saved my life. You've crowned me with love and mercy. You satisfy my every desire with good things. You've supercharged my life so that I soar again like a flying eagle in the sky!

Psalms 103:3-5 TPT

"We're only as close to God as we choose to be."

–*Tuwana Nicole*

Chapter 10

Lust of the Flesh

*Do not love the world or anything in the world. If anyone loves the world, love for the Father is not in them. For everything in the world-**the lust of the flesh**, the lust of the eyes, and the pride of life-comes not from the Father but from the world. The world and its desires pass away, but whoever does the will of God lives forever.*

1 John 2:15-17 NIV

Because I was the product of an adulterous relationship, the enemy used my birth to condemn me before my life could truly begin. I felt there was no way I could ever be accepted by God. Rejection was deeply rooted in me since I was a baby. Because I doubted God from the beginning, the enemy always used my desire to be loved as the main portal to lead me into sin.

The lust of flesh has been the most difficult for me to overcome because I was still operating from a place of rejection from people even after I rededicated my life to God in 2009. Even though I believed that God loved me, I still desired the love of a man. I would always tell God that I needed a human man to love me too.

Lured In Again

Every time I would get to a place of being content in my relationship with God, someone would come along and ask, "Why is a young lady as pretty as you still single?" Though I know they didn't mean any harm, it would open the door to my desire to find companionship from a man outside of my contentment with the MAN (God). So I found myself on the lookout for a husband again.

The enemy used my ignorance of who God really is to lead me into a continual cycle of relationships with men looking for God in them. They were just wanting somebody, anybody to love them too. I had been celibate for a number of years, but I was still so hung up on getting a husband that I spent many years seeking to be loved by a man until the beginning of 2016. I made the decision to marry myself, feeling that I was enough. I didn't need anyone to love me when I love myself. Though there was nothing wrong with me loving myself, God has placed an innate need inside of each of us that can only be fulfilled by Him. I would soon find out this truth.

In 2017, I finally began to become completely content in my relationship with myself and God. But, In August of that same year, God told me that my husband was coming. God told me to get prepared. I thought I was prepared until he showed up. In the beginning, everything was great. He seemed very spiritual and I really thought that this was someone that I could spend my life with. Soon the enemy began to slither in and next thing you know, I had given in to the lust of the flesh again. I had begun to fall back into my old ways.

From Rejected to Redeemed

For the flesh desires what is contrary to the Spirit, and the Spirit what is contrary to the flesh. They are in conflict with each other, so that you are not to do whatever you want.

Galatians 5:17 NIV

Since I had failed the test, the enemy began to have a field's day with me. I wasted a whole year trying to fight my desires and grasp why God had told me that my husband was coming and this man was my husband. My instability was coming from my fleshly desires to have a man and my desire for a relationship with God too. I was torn between the soul tie I had created and the lover of my soul!

An indecisive man is unstable in all his ways.

James 1:8 HCSB

A lot of what causes us to be double minded is our desire for the things of the world and our desire for what God is offering. Many times we want the hand of God, without seeking His face. By this time I knew that God loved me and I also knew that I was made in His image. I knew my purpose (all that God had revealed up this time) and I knew that God had said that my husband was coming. I was torn between allowing my flesh to lead or waiting on God to give me the next step. By this time I simply wanted a husband to successfully do the work that God had called me to do. He was the closest thing so I thought to what I wanted and what I needed.

Have you ever noticed how the enemy will lure you in then leave you to fend for yourself? That's exactly what happened. After playing on the devil's playground for a minute, I literally ended up getting burnt! Instead of allowing God to treat me, I allowed the enemy to trick me out! So here I am in the grips of the enemy again and I had a decision to make. I had been crying out to God for months in regard to this trap that the enemy had set for me. All the while, it was simply another test from God to show the enemy where my loyalty was. I had to decide whether I wanted God more than I wanted a man. I had gone down this road too many times by now, so I knew that God's way was the best way! I chose God!

For your Creator will be your husband; the Lord of Heaven's Armies is his name! He is your Redeemer, the Holy One of Israel, the God of all the earth.

Isaiah 54:5 NLT

Revelation Moment

I am so thankful that God had told me to begin preparing for my husband. He told me to prepare by fasting and praying. Those were the only two things that kept me from being overtaken by the craftiness of the enemy seducing me with the illusion that I would finally have a husband that I could do ministry with. Because sin is so pleasurable, it leads to a lifestyle of over indulgence and separation from God. So we must always pray to keep the flesh from getting weak.

"Watch and pray so that you will not fall into temptation. The spirit is willing, but the flesh is weak."

Matthew 26:41 NIV

Making the decision to marry God was one of the most painful, yet rewarding tests that I had to pass since rededicating my life back to God after the murder my Mother. I thought that God had quenched the deepest desires of my heart when I found myself at His feet in 2008, but now I realize that I was simply scratching the surface of who God is. There are levels to knowing God and I was at the beginning of my understanding.

From Rejected to Redeemed

Only God could truly satisfy the deepest longings of my soul. All this time I was thinking that a man in the flesh was going to help me finally complete God's plan for my life, but God was taking me to another reality of who He is. God was the husband that was coming. I had to allow God to be the head of my life so I could understand the true purpose of marriage. God needed to change my perspective on marriage so I would never put a man above my relationship with Him ever again!

I understand that God ordains marriage and even created woman as a suitable helper for man (Genesis 2:18-25). However, we cannot get ahead of God and choose our own mate. Adam didn't choose Eve and neither should we. Because marriage mirrors our relationship with God, it is very important to be walking in obedience to God in order to have a successful marriage.

This decision brought me one step closer to overcoming rejection. I finally passed the flesh test! I always thought that this would be something I would struggle with for the rest of my life or until I got married. But by continuing the process of redemption, I am allowing God to renew my mind so I can learn what is pleasing to Him (Romans 12:2).

God has proven Himself faithful, showing me that no one can ever fill the position that is only intended for Him to fulfill (Exodus 34:14) So now I no longer attempt to put a man on a pedestal. I realize that pedestal is reserved only for God!

"When you play on the devil's playground you will get burnt."

-Tuwana Nicole

Chapter 11

Lust of the Eyes

*Do not love the world or anything in the world. If anyone loves the world, love for the Father is not in them. For everything in the world-the lust of the flesh, **the lust of the eyes**, and the pride of life-comes not from the Father but from the world. The world and its desires pass away, but whoever does the will of God lives forever.*

1 John 2:15-17 NIV

The world uses images, videos, movies, ads, and billboards to get our attention. It's not very hard for our eyes to deceive us because the world makes everything look good. It's very important that we guard what we allow our eyes to focus on. Sometimes all it takes is one look that leads us down an insidious path that is almost impossible to recover from.

I grew up in a lot of dysfunction so it was very easy for me to look at other people's lives and wish that it was my life. I always wanted the love of my Father, so every time I saw another little girl with her Daddy; I longed for it. Even though desiring a Father in and of itself wasn't sinful, but it opened up the door for me to look for a Father in every boy/man that I met as I grew up.

Our Desires Cloud Our Judgment

The eyes of your spirit allow revelation-light to enter into your being. If your heart is unclouded, the light floods in! But if your eyes are focused on money, the light cannot penetrate and darkness takes its place. How profound will be the darkness within you if the light of truth cannot enter!

Matthew 6:22-23 TPT

Because I grew up with a deep desire to experience the love of my Father, it made it almost impossible for me to ever see God as my Father. The enemy used my clouded judgment to continue to shift my focus away from God. I attempted to fulfill my desire to have a picture perfect life by pursuing a successful career. By pursuing success, I thought everything else would fall into place. I believed relationship status would lead me to the picture perfect life that I so desperately desired. I had allowed my desires to cloud my judgment so I couldn't fully come out of darkness.

Satan, who is the god of this world has blinded the minds of those who don't believe. They are unable to see the glorious light of the Good News. They don't understand this message about the glory of Christ, who is the exact likeness of God.

2 Corinthians 4:4 TPT

Revelation Moment

Because Satan is the god of the world, what we see is simply an illusion. Once you begin to look more closely, we realize that he's offering is a cheap imitation for what God has to offer. My desires had blinded me from what had already been made available to me through a relationship with God. The enemy used my desires to trick me into thinking that I could get them without God and I ended up with a trick for real.

After repeated attempts to achieve a picture perfect life in my own strength, I realized that I would never achieve it without my Creator (God). It took the murder of my Mother in February 2008 to finally wake me up. As tragic as her death was, I knew she had to die in order for me to truly live. I began to realize that my life is not my own so I would never be able to get it to look the way I always dreamed it to be. I realized that I would have to give up my plan for God's plan.

"By not actively pursuing God, you passively choose to follow the devil."

–Tuwana Nicole

Chapter 12

Pride of Life

*Do not love the world or anything in the world. If anyone loves the world, love for the Father is not in them. For everything in the world-the lust of the flesh, the lust of the eyes, and **the pride of life**-comes not from the Father but from the world. The world and its desires pass away, but whoever does the will of God lives forever.*

1 John 2:15-17 NIV

Pride is defined as a feeling of deep pleasure or satisfaction derived from one's own achievements. Pride is so ingrained in our society that most wouldn't even consider it to be an issue. Everywhere you look, you see country pride, school pride, church pride, family pride, team pride, work pride, and community pride. You even have many celebrating pride in their sexuality.

Pride is so prevalent in our society that we passively go along with it because it is very subtle. Unfortunately, pride opens the door for the enemy to walk right in because it doesn't acknowledge God as the source of fulfillment. Pride points to self as the source.

Even though I acknowledged God as my Creator and Savior, I didn't acknowledge Him as my source or my Lord because I struggled to see Him as my Father. I had never received the love of a father so at this point in my life, I was still attempting to be the god of my own life. Since my success in life depended on me and me alone, the enemy sat back and watched my life spiral out of control for the perfect opportunity to completely possess (demonize) me.

I would always pray and ask God to direct my path, but as soon as things didn't go the way I thought they should go, I would complain to God. Then I would turn around and do what I wanted to do. I never would acknowledge if this was something that God wanted me to do or if what I was doing was within His will for my life. Pride is directly contrary to the character of God. My pride would not allow me to humble myself to God.

Pride leads to disgrace, but with humility comes wisdom.

Proverbs 11:2 NLT

Pride in Possessions

Don't keep hoarding for yourselves earthly treasures that can be stolen by thieves. Material wealth eventually rusts, decays, and loses its value. Instead, stockpile heavenly treasures for yourselves that cannot be stolen and will never rust, decay, or lose their value. For your heart will always pursue what you value as your treasure. "How could you worship two gods at the same time? You will have to hate one and love the other, or be devoted to one and despise the other. You can't worship the true God while enslaved to the god of money!

Matthew 6:19-21, 24 TPT

All the things that the world pursues: Wealth, power, status, fame, domination all lead to collapse because they are rooted in selfishness. I realized that since I had never truly accepted God as my Father, I had allowed the pride of life to fuel my decision making. I had always taken pride in being a

successful teenage mother, graduating with honors from high school, getting scholarships to college without student loans, obtaining a successful career, buying a home, getting a nice car, and ultimately getting the man of my dreams!
By pursuing what the world pursues, I was slowing being enslaved by the pride of life.

The Pride Test

*One day the angels came to present themselves before the Lord, and Satan also came with them. The Lord said to Satan, "Where have you come from?" Satan answered the Lord, "From roaming throughout the earth, going back and forth on it." Then the Lord said to Satan, "**Have you considered my servant Job?** There is no one on earth like him; he is blameless and upright, a man who fears God and shuns evil." "Does Job fear God for nothing?" Satan replied. "Have you not put a hedge around him and his household and everything he has? You have blessed the work of his hands, so that his flocks and herds are spread throughout the land. **But now stretch out your hand and strike everything he has, and he will surely curse you to your face.**" The Lord said to Satan, "Very well, then, everything he has is in your power, but on the man himself do not lay a finger." Then Satan went out from the presence of the Lord.*

Job 1:6-12 NIV

After the murder of my Mother, I never returned back to my corporate job. God allowed me heal from my loss and begin to come into who He had always intended for me to be. I was experiencing the miraculous through the ministry God has called me to. Money would show up in my bank account that I wasn't expecting. I would receive favor with businesses to receive donations. God gave me ideas to raise money to keep the shelter afloat. I would be able to buy things at a substantial discount. It seemed that I had finally arrived.

Shortly after losing my health, I struggled to maintain all the possessions that I had acquired over the years. By this time I had been walking with God about four years and had committed my life to serving Him. Things seemed to improve after I received the first settlement from the insurance company. I felt on top of the world.

It seemed my health and my finances were improving when all of a sudden out of nowhere I began to feel a nudge from God to give up my house. That was not only shocking to hear, but it was not something that I wanted to do. Because I had always taken pride in how well I had balanced my life, the last thing that I wanted to do was show any more signs of defeat. I frantically started looking for another house that I could afford with the settlement that I had received from my car crash.

Still operating with pride, I made a hasty decision to purchase a condo from a man that God had already shown me was crooked in his dealings. I met him when I was assisting a client that he was evicting. I was trying to help her keep her apartment, but he was very cold hearted and did not want to work with her. Instead of seeing this as a warning from God, even ignoring the advice of my realtor (who was attempting to protect me), I went head first into this partnership without acknowledging how God was leading me. To make matters worse, I went and bought a brand new car. Because I wanted to save face and maintain my integrity, I wasted the resources that God had blessed me with.

Revelation Moment

I ended up losing the condo within two years after God told me to give up my dream home. Within a few months, my new custom built car was being repossessed. Because I wasn't quite ready to get to the end of myself again, God forced me to see that I was still prideful and wasn't allowing Him to lead.

Then Jesus went to work on his disciples. Anyone who intends to come with me has to let me lead. You're not in the driver's seat; I am. Don't run from suffering; embrace it. Follow me and I'll show you how.

Matthew 16:24 MSG

At that moment, I realized that I wasn't allowing God to lead every aspect of my life. Because I was not ready for deliverance, I began to slip back into depression and my previous sin behavior because I still wanted to control my life. My disobedience and rebellion against God stunted my growth for almost three years because I wanted what I wanted!

Even though God allowed the enemy to take my possessions, it was pride that almost made me forfeit God's plan for my life. I had to make a decision to stay on the losing team and be eternally damned like Satan or to humble myself and try God's way again!

"The enemy comes to steal your focus and kill your relationship with God."

–Tuwana Nicole

Chapter 13

Deny God

*They claim to know God, but by their
actions they deny Him. They are disgusting,
disobedient, and disqualified from doing
anything good.*

Titus 1:16 TPT

We know from the beginning in the Garden of Eden
that Satan used the temptation to doubt God by
changing one word that God has already spoken.
He always uses doubt when we are unsure of who we
are (in our infancy physically or spiritually). He
knows that if he can make us doubt, then he can
make us deny what God has spoken, deny God, then
we ultimately disobey God.

Because Satan rebelled against God and was cast
out of heaven and is eternally damned, he wants us
to forfeit our inheritance too! He wants us to do just
like Adam and Eve; take matters into their own
hands to become wise in your own eyes instead of
waiting on God to give us wisdom. What he doesn't
let us in on is that if we ask God for wisdom, He will
freely give it to us.

*And if anyone longs to be wise, ask God for wisdom
and he will give it! He won't see your lack of wisdom
as an opportunity to scold you over your failures
but he will overwhelm your failures with his
generous grace.*

James 1:5 TPT

The enemy makes us believe that following God's Way
is too hard and that we can get what we need without

God. We put on the mask of independence and begin thinking we can acquire wisdom on our own. The enemy gives us false ideas and we begin saying things like, "I have already been to church this week" or "That's enough about God." Or "Enough about God, what about me?" or "Enough about God, now let's party." or "Ok...ok...I know God is good, but_____."

(fill in the blank)

The enemy will always make us believe that whatever we do in the name of Jesus will be pleasing to God. He will make us feel like we can do things that are contrary to the will of God or accomplish things without God's authority, then justify our behavior by claiming it in the name of Jesus with our mouths.

"These people honor me with their lips, but their heart is far from me. They worship me in vain, teaching as doctrines the commands of men."

Matthew 15:8-9 HCSB

The enemy comes for us so hard that we don't know if we're coming or going. He will stop at nothing to get us to deny God. He is relentless in his quest. Because Satan is the god of this world, he wants us to become the god of our world!

*Then their mind changes and they transgress and commit offense; **their own power is their god.***

Habakkuk 1:11 MEV

Because we want to have God and have our own way, we keep taking the enemy's bait and get caught in his trap. The devil has many of us thinking it's our haters, our relationships, and our money; but we don't see that his real strategy is to dilute our minds and make us ultimately deny God. Once the enemy has successfully deceived us into denying God's way, we begin pursuing self, and become our own god.

Revelation Moment

Denial of God always leads to a dead end, disappointment, and oftentimes self-destruction if we don't turn and repent. We see this happen time and time again throughout the scriptures with the children of Israel, King Saul, Nebuchadnezzar, Saul, Peter, and many others who chose to deny God.

Even in our denial of God, He still has given us an example to help us come to repentance. Jesus knew that Peter would deny Him three times so He explained to him the importance of his repentance. Peter's repentance was vital to the Kingdom of God and for others to come into the knowledge of who God is.

*""Peter, my dear friend, listen to what I'm about to tell you. **Satan has obtained permission to come and sift you all like wheat and test your faith.** But I have prayed for you, Peter, that you would stay faithful to me no matter what comes. **Remember this: after you have turned back to me and have been restored, make it your life mission to strengthen the faith of your brothers.**" "But Lord," Peter replied, "I am ready to stand with you to the very end, even if it means prison or death!" Jesus looked at him and prophesied, "**Before the rooster crows in the morning, you will deny three times that you even know me.**""*

Luke 22:31-34 TPT

When I began to look back over my life, I realized that I had done just like Peter and many others. I had denied God with my actions. Though I worshipped God with my mouth, I always put self-preservation above God. So even if I was wrong and needed repentance, I couldn't see it if it meant me humbling myself. It took me denying Jesus at least three times before I came to the revelation that I could not do what I wanted to do and still be a child of God.

The whole idea of believing that we can do life on our own or figure life out on our own terms is not possible without God. Once I finally understood that I didn't create myself, so there was no way that I could deny my Creator. Once I began to believe in God and accept Him as the only voice of wisdom, He has accomplished things through me that I never thought were possible. Once you're on this journey, then and only then will you be empowered to do what God has intended for you to do!

"The Enemy lures, but God draws."

–Tuwana Nicole

Part 3

How to Overcome the Plan of the Enemy

Overcome is defined as success in dealing with a problem or difficulty.

In fact, this is love for God: to keep his commands. And his commands are not burdensome, for everyone born of God overcomes the world. This is the victory that has overcome the world, even our faith. Who is it that overcomes the world? Only the one who believes that Jesus is the Son of God.

1 John 5:3-5 NIV

Chapter 14

Let Jesus Redeem You

But as for me, God will redeem my life. He will snatch me from the power of the grave.

Psalms 49:15 NLT

Redeem is defined as to gain or regain possession of something in exchange for payment. That is exactly what Jesus did when He rose from the dead on the third day with all power in His hands. Jesus redeemed us from the power of the grave. Jesus redeemed us from the sting of death. Jesus redeemed us from our sins. Jesus redeemed us from the old person we used to be!

Since the beginning of time, the enemy has been using the same tactics to make us forfeit God's plan for our lives. God created a way for us to escape the plan of the enemy by sending His son Jesus Christ to reconcile us back to Himself. When Jesus was resurrected, we were resurrected with Him! So when Jesus overcame death, we overcame death too! When Jesus defeated the plan of Satan, our enemy; we defeated his plan too!

"From this moment on, everything in this world is about to change, for the ruler of this dark world will be overthrown. And I will do this when I am lifted up off the ground and when I draw the hearts of people to gather them to me."

John 12:31-33 TPT

How Deep are The Roots?

I knew John 3:16 KJV; *for God so loved the world that he gave his only begotten Son, that whosoever believeth in him should not perish, but have everlasting life.* Because I never knew the love of my earthly Father, I didn't understand the love of my Heavenly Father. I simply came to Jesus out of religious obligation and fear at the age 13. So the enemy came in and took what little understanding I had.

The seed that fell on the footpath represents those who hear the message about the Kingdom and don't understand it. Then the evil one comes and snatches away the seed that was planted in their hearts.

Matthew 13:19 NLT

My encounter with Jesus at the age of 33 has changed the entire trajectory of my life. For the first time I could see the loving nature of God.

"But-When God our Savior revealed his kindness and love, he saved us, not because of the righteous things we had done, but because of his mercy. He washed away our sins, giving us a new birth and new life through the Holy Spirit. He generously poured out the Spirit upon us through Jesus Christ our Savior. Because of his grace he made us right in his sight and gave us confidence that we will inherit eternal life."

Titus 3:4-7 NLT

Even though this encounter with Jesus was very significant and I had many awesome experiences and growth in my relationship with God. I realized that when my pride was tested after my car crash, I wasn't as deeply rooted as I thought I was. I loved God and I knew He loved me. I had produced some fruit by accepting my calling to ministry to share God's love with others, but I had only recognized Jesus' love for me. I still hadn't learned how to love myself or how much the pride of life influenced many of my decisions, even how I initially did the work of the ministry God has called me to.

*The seed on the rocky soil represents those who hear the message and **immediately receive it with joy. But since they don't have deep roots, they don't last long.** They fall away as soon as they have problems or are persecuted for believing God's word. The seed that fell among the thorns represents those who hear God's word, but all too quickly **the message is crowded out by the worries of this life and the lure of wealth, so no fruit is produced.***

Matthew 13:20-22 NLT

I struggled over a period of about three years where I didn't produce much fruit. I had slipped back into my old habits of trying to figure out how I was going to make a living and find a husband. I went through several significant attacks from the enemy because I didn't follow all of God's instructions.

I entered into business deals, partnered with ministries, and entered into relationships with men that God told me not to engage in. I even attempted to marry myself as if that was going to get me out of the ditch I dug for myself. At this point I still didn't understand how the pride of life was so deeply rooted in me. God was using the devil to test me to bring me back into His will so I could fulfill the purpose He has for my life.

The punishment you brought me through was the best thing that could have happened to me, for it taught me your ways.

Psalms 119:71 TPT

After I had suffered for a little while God, told me to get back focused on Him. He reminded me of Job again. He told me to go back and read Job 42. God revealed again that His plan for my life cannot be stopped no matter what comes against me. He showed me that His will for my life will prevail. I have been more fruitful for the Kingdom of God in the past two years than I had been in all of the previous years combined. I will discuss that more in later chapters.

The seed that fell on good soil represents those who truly hear and understand God's word and produce a harvest of thirty, sixty, or even a hundred times as much as had been planted!

Matthew 13:23 NLT

God sends some storms to perfect our faith. He had allowed me to suffer so I would seek Him and seek Him only! God wanted to be the only fertilizer for my faith! God wanted to ensure that He got the glory for my life! I was never able to fully articulate this revelation until after I passed the lust of the flesh test.

There is Only 1 Choice

Today I am giving you a choice. You can choose life and success or death and disaster. I am commanding you to be loyal to the LORD, to live the way he has told you, and to obey his laws and teachings. If you obey him, you will live and become successful and powerful. On the other hand, you might choose to disobey the LORD and reject him. So I'm warning you that if you bow down and worship other gods, you won't have long to live.

Deuteronomy 30:15-16, 18 CEVUK

This scripture pretty much sums it up. There are only 2 choices, but prayerfully by now you recognize that God is the only choice. What we want to choose or what we are lured in to choose only leads to destruction. God is our Creator so He always wants us to want what He has purposed for us. Many times we go through life thinking that what we want is what's most important when in fact, we can only get what we want by choosing God. Oftentimes as we learn who we really are, we realize that what we originally wanted was simply a substitute for our soul's true desire. Our soul always desires to be reunited with its Creator. St. Augustine said it best, "A man will never find true happiness until he finds it in the ONE who created him." You can replace the word happiness with love, career, success, wisdom, or whatever you feel that you need in order to finally arrive. You will never fully arrive at any destination without God being in the driver's seat! As long as I ran from the refining fire of God, I was always burned by the crafty ways of the enemy.

Trust the Process

Trust in the Lord with all your heart and do not lean on your own understanding; in all your ways acknowledge Him, and He will direct your paths.

Proverbs 3:5-6 MEV

If the enemy cannot get you to choose his plan, then he will try to make you think that you need to have it all together as soon as you accept Jesus to be your personal Lord and Savior. But don't let that discourage you. Now that we know how the enemy infiltrates the church through religion/denominationalism. We must be aware of the demands that may be placed on us.

If you grew up in a religious system like I did, you are learning that religion doesn't save. Remember religion condemns, but the Holy Spirit convicts. Religion wants you to feel guilty, but God wants you to trust Him. Some things you can get through instantaneously and some things are a process. As you continue to develop your relationship with God, you will see yourself becoming more of who God intended you to be. Sometimes it doesn't make sense, but when God is in it, you can trust the process.

Be willing to die the death of a caterpillar so we can become a butterfly for the Kingdom of God. The metamorphosis (to transform or change) process for a butterfly has 4 stages. I hope you can see the correlation between the 4 stages of the caterpillar and the 4 soils. The 4 stages are:

1. **Egg/New Convert**-is the new believer who just received the Word. This is the stage where it is vital for a new believer to be planted in a Bible believing community so that they can be fed. Matthew 13:19
2. **Larva/Baby Believer**-is the growing caterpillar or spiritual baby needing lots of milk to be able to begin maturing. There should be massive growth during this stage if they are firmly planted in the right place. Matthew 13:20-21
3. **Pupa/Maturing Believer**-represents the transformation from a caterpillar into the butterfly within a shell (cocoon) or the baby believer going from immaturity to maturity. This is the stage where many believe that nothing is happening or that God isn't working. This can be a very difficult time as it requires us to completely die to self. This is typically a season of preparation for the greater that God wants to do. Some people refer to it as the secret place with God. This is the stage that many give up because it's the most painful. Matthew 13:22
4. **Adult/Mature Believer**-represents the butterfly that is fully mature breaking out of its shell (cocoon) able to produce fruit and lead others to Christ. This is a time of increased fruitfulness for the Kingdom. There may be many travels to different cities, states, and nations to lead others to Christ. Matthew 13:23

This process is a lifelong process for the butterfly and for us too.. The only difference is the butterfly's life cycle is much shorter than most of ours. Once the process is complete, we go through the process again. But the 2nd, 3rd, etc. times around we should be wiser and more fruitful in each stage. This process can also represent generations of our families trusting the process too. Just like becoming comfortable in your own skin, the skin that God created for His glory, must be continually shed to be made more in the image of God. But make sure you don't make excuses or you will delay the process or cause death because you are attempting to make it happen yourself instead of allowing the natural progression.

You may not understand why you have to go through the pain, but when you get through to the other side you will understand the process. The process is to prune us, shape us, mold us, and refine us so we can possess everything that God has already promised and prepared for us.

Revelation Moment

The devil may be the god of the world, but God owns the World and everything in it, including us! Just look around at nature and you will see the miracle, wonder working power of God in every aspect of life. Because I still didn't fully understand the importance of allowing God to lead in every area of my life, I realized that I was just like Peter. I had denied Jesus three times after initially accepting Him to be my Lord and Savior.

From Rejected to Redeemed

The enemy only has the authority that God gives him. Being that God gives the enemy this authority to test our faith, it is of the utmost importance that we allow Jesus to redeem us from the enemy's authority. We will never be able to fight the enemy in our own strength so let Jesus redeem you! Our parents may have allowed the enemy to stop the metamorphosis process in their lives, but that doesn't mean that we have to. We can get deeper roots by allowing Jesus to redeem us!

*Once you were dead because of your disobedience and your many sins. You used to live in sin, just like the rest of the world, obeying the devil—the commander of the powers in the unseen world. He is the spirit at work in the hearts of those who refuse to obey God. All of us used to live that way, following the passionate desires and inclinations of our sinful nature. By our very nature we were subject to God's anger, just like everyone else. **But God is so rich in mercy, and he loved us so much, that even though we were dead because of our sins, he gave us life when he raised Christ from the dead. (It is only by God's grace that you have been saved!)** For he raised us from the dead along with Christ and seated us with him in the heavenly realms because we are united with Christ Jesus. So God can point to us in all future ages as examples of the incredible wealth of his grace and kindness toward us, as shown in all he has done for us who are united with Christ Jesus. **God saved you by his grace when you believed.** And you can't take credit for this; it is a gift from God. **Salvation is not a reward for the good things we have done, so none of us can boast about it. For we are God's masterpiece. He has created us anew in Christ Jesus, so we can do the good things he** planned for us long ago.*

Ephesians 2:1-10 NLT

Say this simple prayer:

Dear Lord Jesus,

I thank you for offering me the gift of eternal life. I realize that I did not earn this gift, but today I receive it. I no longer want to live for myself, but I want to live for you. I confess with my mouth that you are my Lord and King. I believe in my heart that you died for my sins and that God raised you from the dead. I receive you into my heart. I thank you for forgiving me of my sins and making me right with you. Teach me to be more like you and to live for you each day.

In your Mighty name I pray,

Amen.

*"O give thanks unto the Lord, for he is good: for **his mercy endureth for ever.** Let the redeemed of the Lord say so, whom **he hath redeemed from the hand of the enemy."***

Psalms 107:1-2 KJV

"Rejection is redirection to feet of Jesus."

-Tuwana Nicole

Chapter 15

Know the Voice of God

"Dear friend, listen well to my words; tune your ears to my voice. Keep my message in plain view at all times. Concentrate! Learn it by heart! Those who discover these words live, really live; body and soul, they're bursting with health."

Proverbs 4:20-22 MSG

Obeying the voice of God once you have accepted Jesus to be your personal Lord and Savior is very vital to overcoming the plan of the enemy. Even though I had been hearing the voice of God since I was a baby, I struggled with believing that God was really speaking to me. My life circumstances overshadowed God's voice so it was easier to be deceived by the lies of the enemy.

In order to truly know the voice of God, we must be able to discern if what we're hearing is from God or from the enemy. The enemy used my ignorance of God and inability to know that God's way is best for me. The enemy constantly bombarded my mind with negative thoughts to drown out God's voice making me believe that because I had been born into sin, I was destined to live a life of sin, and would ultimately die in my sins!

Looking back now, we can understand why the enemy attacks us in our infancy as a child, but also our infancy as a believer. Satan's job is to always give us the temptation to doubt. He wants us to keep believing the lie that we can get whatever it is we desire without

God. If we always doubt God, we will never truly listen to God let alone obey His voice.

Now that you have allowed Jesus to redeem you, you should be beginning to see that God really loves us. He not only went to great lengths to redeem us, He is very serious about us being able to discern His voice from the shouts of the enemy.

After finding myself at the feet of Jesus, but still continuing to have the desire to revisit places that I thought I was delivered from made it evident that my mind had been diluted by the enemy for a very long time. I had become so accustomed to believing his lies that I kept falling prey to his tactics. I knew God loved me, but I did more trying rather than simply trusting God at this point in my life.

Childlike Faith

Learn this well: Unless you dramatically change your way of thinking and become teachable, and learn about heaven's kingdom realm with the wide-eyed wonder of a child, you will never be able to enter in. Whoever continually humbles himself to become like this gentle child is the greatest one in heaven's kingdom realm.

Matthew 18:3-4 TPT

Children are very trusting and dependent on their parents and those who care for them. They don't worry if their needs are going to be taken care of or concern themselves with anything. They simply trust and believe that all of their needs are going to be met daily by their parents. Children are naturally honest and speak truthfully. They don't have a motive to lie. They see the world exactly as it is and obey the voice of God to bring correction to it by speaking the truth. Now that we are children of God, it's important that we know His voice. Not only is it important to know His voice, but be willing to obey His voice too! If you have experienced a lot of childhood trauma like I have, you never really learned how to trust the voice of God. But we must be diligent to trust God's voice with childlike faith in spite of our past.

The devil could care less that we can hear God's voice just like he could care less that we go to church or are religious. What's important to the enemy is that we never really find out who we are so he will keep us distracted or keep haunting us with our past so we never get around to understanding that if we delight ourselves in the Lord, He will give us the desires of our heart (Psalms 37:4).

God is a Speaking God

And we know [with great confidence] that God [who is deeply concerned about us] causes all things to work together [as a plan] for good for those who love God, to those who are called according to His plan and purpose. For those whom He foreknew [and loved and chose beforehand], He also predestined to be conformed to the image of His Son [and ultimately share in His complete sanctification], so that He would be the firstborn [the most beloved and honored] among many believers. And those whom He predestined, He also called; and those whom He called, He also justified [declared free of the guilt of sin]; and those whom He justified, He also glorified [raising them to a heavenly dignity]."

ROMANS 8:28-30 AMP

God, the Creator of the Heavens and the Earth has been speaking since the beginning of time. He spoke everything He created into existence. I knew the voice of God before I knew it was His voice. God allowed my car crash to bring me back into remembrance of who I truly am to Him. God allowed me to lose some unimportant memories so I could remember the most important memory! God wanted me to remember His purpose and plan for my life. God wanted me to remember HIM!

Now it makes sense why God has been speaking to me since I was a baby. God spoke to me like He did Jeremiah. God told me that He had a purpose for my life, for me to be a prophet to the nations (Jeremiah 1:5). Just like God spoke me into existence, He spoke me into existence for such a time as this knowing exactly what I would go through and who He has purposed me to be. God allowed me to go through so I could learn to trust Him to get me through.

God speaks to us so we will know who we are to Him. We know by now that the enemy attacks us in every area of life so that we won't believe that we are who God says that we are. God doesn't give us all the details about how we are going to become who He said that we are, but He wants us to trust Him and leave the how up to Him.

Actively Listen

So listen, my child. Don't reject correction or you will certainly wander from the ways of truth.

Proverbs 19:27 TPT

That's why it's important to become like children and allow God to retrain our minds so we can not only hear His voice, but learn to trust that He knows what's best for us. We can't be a child of God and stay the same. If we keep the same pattern of thinking even after allowing Jesus to redeem us, we will remain easy prey for the enemy.

After being led astray so many times, I realized that I was still trying instead of trusting God. I was leaning on my own understanding instead of acknowledging God in all ways so He could direct my path (Proverbs 3:5). If you're not teachable, you're not humble. If you don't listen to the voice of God, you will continue to reject His leading and remain an easy target for the enemy. It may seem backwards in our world that promotes independence, but in the Kingdom of God dependence is essential for optimal growth.

When we stay at the feet of Jesus like a little child that hangs on to every word that our Daddy speaks, we won't miss what He wants us to know. God is always speaking to us, but if we are consumed by everything that is going on around us, we won't be able to hear His instructions. We cannot allow the distractions that the enemy uses to keep us from actively listening and obeying the voice of God.

Revelation Moment

You are my satisfaction, Lord, and all that I need, so I'm determined to do everything you say.

Psalms 119:57 TPT

The more we allow our faith to arise, the more we realize that having childlike faith is truly the key to always being able to hear God's voice, actively listen, and experience the abundant life through obedience. As long as I thought I had all the answers, my thoughts and the shouts of the world overpowered the voice of God. I began to realize that I could only hear God clearly as I continued to surrender my will to His Will. So instead of worrying about what God is going to do next, I obey God in the moment and then I watch Him bless the next.

Many don't understand what I'm doing and I must admit that many times I don't even understand where God is leading me. But God always knows what He is doing so I trust Him and continue to walk by faith no matter how crazy it may seem in the eyesight of man. I'm constantly giving up the good so I, my children, my children's children, and you and your children can have the great! No matter where God leads me, I know it's for my good and for His glory!

"Don't Try, Trust God"

-Tuwana Nicole

Chapter 16

Get Battle Ready

A final word: Be strong in the Lord and in his mighty power. **Put on all of God's armor so that you will be able to stand firm against all strategies of the devil.** *For we are not fighting against flesh-and-blood enemies, but against evil rulers and authorities of the unseen world, against mighty powers in this dark world, and against evil spirits in the heavenly places. Therefore,* **put on every piece of God's armor so you will be able to resist the enemy in the time of evil.** *Then after the battle you will still be standing firm. Stand your ground, putting on the* **belt of truth and the body armor of God's righteousness.** *For shoes, put on the peace that comes from the Good News so that you will be fully prepared. In addition to all of these, hold up the* **shield of faith** *to stop the fiery arrows of the devil. Put on salvation as your helmet, and take the* **sword of the Spirit,** *which is the word of God. Pray in the Spirit at all times and on every occasion. Stay alert and be persistent in your prayers for all believers everywhere."*

Ephesians 6:10-18 NLT

Armor is defined as coverings worn by soldiers or warriors to protect the body during a battle or defense system. Now that we have identified that we have a real unseen enemy, why we are his target, and how he operates; it is of the utmost importance that we get battle ready so we can overcome him. Because we are made in the image of God and understand His purpose for our lives, Satan and his angels are going to come hard for us. We must get prepared and fight with the armor and in the strength of the Lord. So we must be on guard for the little foxes (Song of Songs 2:15 TPT). The little foxes are all of the schemes of the enemy to steal, kill, and destroy our relationship with God.

Soldiers for the Kingdom

For every soldier called to active duty must divorce himself from the distractions of this world so that he may fully satisfy the one who chose him.

2 Timothy 2:4 TPT

When we made the decision to allow Jesus to redeem us, we became a soldier in the Army of the Lord. As a soldier for Christ, we must make sure that we have on the full armor of God so the enemy cannot penetrate our lives and catch us by surprise. We must continue to realize that the enemy runs the world so as a soldier for Christ we must keep our focus on our commanding officer, Jesus Christ. We cannot concern ourselves with the things of this world, we must be singular focused and understand what our mission is.

When we put on the full armor of God, we will be properly equipped to rescue those who have been imprisoned by the enemy. We will be able to stand firm and win battles against the evil that is all around us. With the full armor of God on, we begin to realize that the power of evil around us is no match for the power of Jesus within us.

The Whole Armor of God

Belt of Truth (verse 14)-The only way to mitigate the lies of the enemy is to stand your ground and put on the belt of truth. We have to not only know the voice of God, but we must also trust and obey what God has told us so we won't be deceived by the cunning words of the enemy.

Breastplate of Righteousness (verse 14)-We put on the breastplate by looking like our Commanding Officer, Jesus Christ. Walking in obedience to His way, not living for ourselves. The breastplate symbolizes that we are in right standing with God.

Feet Planted (verse 15)-No matter what shoes we need to fill, our feet will be fitting to fulfill whatever position God needs us to fill as we carry the Good News of Jesus' redeeming power. You become firmly planted when we not only know, but obey the Word of God. When we are firmly planted, it won't be easy to move us from our positioning in Christ.

Shield of Faith (verse 16)-The shield protects us from the flaming arrows of the enemy that are meant to burn us. We will only know develop the shield when we are sure of who we are and Whose we are. Our faith will shield us from fire that enemy sets in an attempt to destroy us.

Helmet of Salvation (verse 17)-By accepting Jesus as our Lord and Savior, we are putting on the helmet of salvation to protect our mind. The enemy will always attempt to attack our minds, but if we keep our helmet on at all times; the enemy won't be able to penetrate our thoughts.

Sword of the Spirit (verse 17)-The Word of God is so important to help us to slay anything that comes against what God has promised for His people. The sword will ward off every demonic attack to our mind, body, and soul! If we keep our swords sharp, the enemy won't stand a chance against us (Proverbs 27:17).

Prayer (verse 18)-When we are missing pieces of our armor, we leave ourselves open to the attacks of the enemy. Prayer is the most powerful piece of armor that we can wear. Without it, we won't see how the enemy is coming. We won't know his plans. It will be easy for us to fall asleep because many times we won't be praying for our fellow soldiers. If we're praying one for another, we will be able to alert each other and keep each other updated and refreshed.

Beware of Friendly Fire

But if you are always biting and devouring one another, watch out! Beware of destroying one another.

Galatians 5:15 NLT

Beware of the plot of the enemy to make us turn on one another. Since we are not fighting against things that we can see with the natural eye, we need to make sure that don't make each other casualties of war by attacking each other. To be battle ready, we must make sure that we are unified and attack the problem, not each other. We cannot allow the enemy to pick us off by pitting us against one another through division.

We are on the same team. We may have different responsibilities, but it requires each of us to get battle ready so we can be prepared for the inevitable attacks. It is of the utmost importance that we work together through the leading of the Holy Spirit, keeping our spiritual eyes open. If we choose to fight each other, we will be ineffective in preventing him from penetrating our defense system.

Stay on the Defense

And don't give the devil an opportunity.

Ephesians 4:27 HCSB

In the game of basketball, it's been said that offense wins games, but defense wins championships. Well I firmly believe that to be true when it comes to the devil. It is clear by now that he is very crafty and cunning. So it is of the utmost importance to always stay on the defense and be prepared for whatever he throws our way. We must keep our eyes open and be quick on our feet.

Before we were thinking about him, he already had a plan in place to destroy us before we could come to know who we are. If we continue to go through life not understanding how he operates, he will turn all of our offensive efforts into another one of his games. We will turn over the ball, get ran out of bounds, knocked on our faces, get dunked on, scored on, get the ball stolen, fouled, fouled out of the game, and ultimately he hopes to get us ejected from the game and lose the championship (Crown of Life).

Rest in Jesus

If we want to stay battle ready, it is important for us to understand that we need to learn how to rest in Jesus. When we get weary, we tend to want to take off our armor. But taking off our armor opens us back up to the attacks of the enemy. This is why it is so important for us to only take on what God wants us to take on so we are not overloaded with burdens that God didn't intend for us to bear.

We are born into this worldly system that tells us to go through life totally opposite of what God intends. It tells us to go, go, go! The only time we get to rest is maybe when we take a vacation. We must learn to allow Jesus to continually refresh us.

This world tells us to:

❖ Go to school
❖ Get a job
❖ Get married
❖ Go to church

Please understand that there is absolutely nothing wrong with pursuing any of these things. The problem is pursuing them in our own strength and without the direction of God. This is the main reason why we end up wearing the mask of intelligence, the mask of success, the mask of relationship status, the mask of religion, and the mask of independence or all of them.
The mind and body breaking down is God's way of trying to get our attention. God never intended for us to carry our own load. But the enemy will keep shouting, "You only live once", "You gotta do what you got to do, or "You better make it happen."

"Relax and rest, be confident and serene, for the Lord rewards fully those who simply trust in Him."

Psalms 116:7 TPT

Revelation Moment

"But be on your guard. Don't let the sharp edge of your expectation get dulled by parties and drinking and shopping. Otherwise, that Day is going to take you by complete surprise, spring on you suddenly like a trap, for it's going to come on everyone, everywhere, at once. So, whatever you do, don't go to sleep at the switch. Pray constantly that you will have the strength and wits to make it through everything that's coming and end up on your feet before the Son of Man."

Luke 21:34-36 MSG

I realized that I had to take off any and everything that was preventing me from being able to put on the full armor of God. In order to be battle ready, I had to let go of the life that I had planned for myself. I realized that on my best day, I was still losing the battle of life. Despite all my offensive moves, my life was still miserable. Even though I had accepted Jesus as my Savior, I hadn't allowed Him to be my Lord. Making Jesus my Lord, my Commanding Officer was essential to get and stay battle ready.

We get battle ready by staying at the feet of Jesus in the presence of God. We must become prayer warriors. We must understand that without God, we can't win the battle. With God, the victory is already won! So stay in the Word of God and seek God in all things.

We must band together in unity keeping God at the core of everything we do in order to withstand the attacks of the enemy. Instead of remaining slaves to sin, let's become a servant of HIM! There is a blessing in the pressing. As we learn to listen to God's directions and walk in unison with one another, we become an unstoppable Army for the Kingdom of God who keep each other sharpened for every good work on the battlefield.

"No matter how many degrees you achieve if GOD is not the center, you won't WIN life!"

-Tuwana Nicole

(Godwin is my father's last name)

Chapter 17

Prayer & Fasting

After this manner therefore pray ye: Our Father which art in heaven, Hallowed be thy name. Thy kingdom come. Thy will be done in earth, as it is in heaven. Give us this day our daily bread. And forgive us our debts, as we forgive our debtors. And lead us not into temptation, but deliver us from evil: For thine is the kingdom, and the power, and the glory, forever. Amen.

Matthew 6:9-13 KJV

I often hear so many people say they don't know how to pray. We think there is some type of special formula or we need to use elegant words to get our prayers heard. The only example given by Jesus in the Bible is what we call the Lord's prayer. This prayer is very simple, yet is specific enough to cover everything we need to get through our day.

When we pray the Lord's prayer we are calling God down into our circumstances. We don't have to wait until we get to heaven to experience what God has for us, we can experience heaven right here on Earth for our good and for God's glory. We serve a living God. In order for God's will to be done here on Earth, it has to be manifested in our lives. Prayer is our way of communicating with our Heavenly Father. It is our way of building and sustaining our relationship with Him. We know that prayer is vital to overcoming the plan of the enemy.

Don't Worry

Don't be pulled in different directions or worried about a thing. Be saturated in prayer throughout each day, offering your faith-filled requests before God with overflowing gratitude. Tell him every detail of your life, then God's wonderful peace that transcends human understanding, will make the answers known to you through Jesus Christ.

Philippians 4:6-7 TPT

When we pray, we must make sure that we do not worry. We must trust and believe that God will work everything out for our good and His glory. I remember when I used to worry and pray at the same time. It made my life very unproductive. I began to realize that if I was going to pray, then why worry. If God said it, that settles it.

We must also be careful to always have gratitude for the things that God has done because it is pointless to pray if we don't believe that God is faithful to do what He said he would do. When we are grateful and remember the basics of what God has done in our lives, it makes it easier to simply trust that His promises never fail.

Season Your Prayers with Fasting

When you fast, don't let it be obvious, but instead, wash your face and groom yourself and realize that your Father in the secret place is the one who is watching all that you do in secret and will continue to reward you openly. When you fast, don't look like those who pretend to be spiritual. They want everyone to know they're fasting, so they appear in public looking miserable, gloomy, and disheveled. Believe me, they've already received their reward in full.

Matthew 6:16-18 TPT

Fasting is defined as a deliberate abstinence from physical gratification, usually food or anything that is pleasing to the flesh in order to gain more clarity. Over the years I have come to realize that anytime we deny ourselves to draw closer to God, it leaves more room for God to work miraculously in our lives.

I have been fasting almost daily since 2017 by denying myself of food, most forms of entertainment, and any distractions that would keep me from drawing closer to God. Though I had been doing this, I had not realized it until a few months ago when the Holy Spirit instructed me to eat breakfast. Since God had told me to begin fasting for my husband in 2017, it had become a part of my daily life. I saw how fasting has brought me to a level in God that I didn't think would ever become possible (overcoming the lust of the flesh), so I developed a deeper hunger for God that I had never had before.

I knew that if my relationship with God alone could bring me to a place of peace that surpasses all of my understanding, which I had never truly had before. I knew anything was possible as long as I continued to believe.

From Rejected to Redeemed

Jesus said to him, "If you can believe, all things are possible to him who believes."

So He said to them, "This kind can come out by nothing but prayer and fasting."

Mark 9:23, 29 NKJV

Around the same time that I began fasting, God saw my hunger for a deeper relationship with Him. So God prompted me to get back on the wall and to begin praying for others. By understanding that some things could only come out through prayer and fasting and seeing the miraculous happen in my life, I felt led me to pray for my family. Once I began to see the miraculous happen in my family, I felt led to begin praying for friends, other believers, and eventually to everyone even those that I do not know.

Revelation Moment

Through my fasting and prayer, I began to see revival breakout everywhere I went. Fasting and prayer is a very powerful weapon against the kingdom of darkness. So the closer I get to God, the more the devil tries to knock me off God's purpose for my life. The devil uses our ignorance of God against us. So the more we learn about God, the more we realize that the devil is a liar. Prayer will help us know the voice of God better and become vessels of great power.

We're only as close to God as we choose to be. What better way to get closer to God is through direct communication with God in prayer and denying ourselves through fasting? When we learn to rely on God for everything, we get our priorities straight and realize that some things we think we need, we don't. When we start to worry about what we don't have that means we are not spending enough time in prayer. Whenever you start to worry, stop and pray. We must remember that if God is truly the head of our lives, we must give Him total control and trust that He will supply all of our needs. This will help us remember that God not only hears our prayers, but He answers our prayers.

If we stay hungry for God, we will not eat the fruit of darkness and fall into deception. I am learning not to eat anything unless I know that it is God. Prayer and fasting has played a major role in getting me one step closer to overcoming the plan of the enemy. I will continue to pursue my relationship with God like never before. I will stay at the feet of Jesus because I realize that's how I continue to win battles that I had never won before. This will be my plan is to continue pressing on!

"A better than blessed life is a life that is surrendered to Christ."

–Tuwana Nicole

Chapter 18

Surrender is the

Pathway to Freedom

"All who seek to live apart from me will lose it all. But those who let go of their lives for my sake and surrender it all to me will discover true life!"

Matthew 10:39 TPT

Making the decision to change my mind when I found myself at the feet of Jesus in 2008, turned out to be the best decision of my life. It started me on a journey that has led me to my true self, the woman God has purposed for me to be from the beginning of time. Every mind battle, every heartache, every heartbreak has led me to a continual surrendering of my will and into obedience to God.

God is the Perfecter of our faith. We should be getting better, but because we want to follow the world, many of us are getting worse. We're digressing instead of progressing. We must allow the pruning of God if we want continuous growth. We must go to the source and get renewed. If we're going straight to the source, we will not become weary. When we rest and trust in God, we won't lean unto our own understanding. We must allow God to direct our paths daily. If we could get it together on our own, we would've done so by now. Many cannot enter the rest of God because we won't surrender to God.

The Lord is a Good Shepherd

A shepherd is someone that leads or guides sheep. Sheep symbolizes someone that needs to be led. God is the shepherd, and we are His sheep. After spending much of my life trying to figure out which way I should go and not being able to discern the voice of God, and being easily misled by my own desires and falling prey to the plan of the enemy; I knew that I needed to allow God to be my good Shepherd.

I knew I couldn't go wrong if I allowed God to lead me. God kept taking me back to the 23rd Psalm. I have known this psalm since childhood, but around the age of 37 I felt an overwhelming urge to revisit it again. Then after reading it in The Passion Translation (TPT) later, I really began to resonate with it on a deeper level.

*The Lord is my **best friend** and my shepherd. **I always have more than enough.***

Psalms 23:1 TPT

I had struggled my entire life with being able to trust people through the abuse that I experienced as a young child, but also as an adult. I was always being mistreated, manipulated, taken advantage of because of my goodness toward others. I didn't want to allow bitterness to try to creep back in again. God had shown Himself trustworthy my entire life. If I was going to continue on this journey, I realized that I have to continue to live a surrendered life to Christ. By allowing God to become my best friend, my shepherd; I could no longer be led astray. I knew that God would not only provide all of my needs, I began to recognize that He would take care of many of my wants too.

*He offers a **resting place for me** in his **luxurious love**. His tracks take me to an oasis of **peace**, the quiet brook of bliss.*

Psalms 23:2 TPT

Since I was tired of being tired, I began to realize that every time that I obey God my life was easier. I didn't have all the struggles anymore because I had begun resting in Him. I no longer felt the pressure to make things happen, I began to realize that God has already made it happen. All I have to do is to keep following Him. By taking God's rest, my life is much more peaceful. Now I finally love my life because my life is hidden in Christ, the lover of my soul!

*That's where he **restores and revives my life**. He **opens before me pathways** to God's pleasure and **leads me along in his footsteps** of righteousness so that I can **bring honor to his name.***

Psalms 23:3 TPT

By allowing God to restore and revive my soul, I finally began to enjoy my life. I never loved myself in the past. By allowing God to be my good Shepherd, He began to open up a life that I had only dreamed about. I truly feel like a new person (2 Corinthians 5:17). The old me is dead and gone and the new Tuwana has come alive. To top it off, everything that God was bringing me to was for my good and to give Him glory. I never thought that it was possible for my life to bring honor to God's name.

From Rejected to Redeemed

*Lord, even when your path takes me through the valley of deepest darkness, **fear will never conquer me**, for you already have! You **remain close to me and lead me through it all** the way. Your authority is my **strength and my peace**. The **comfort of your love** takes away my fear. I'll **never be lonely**, for you are near.*

Psalms 23:4 TPT

Every time the enemy would get me caught up, he would leave me, but God will never leave nor forsake me! No matter what I go through, I know that I can get through ANYTHING because God is leading me. God's presence gives me strength to endure and peace that surpasses all understanding. I am truly comfortable in my own skin because I know God loves me with an everlasting love. No more lonely and fearful nights because the lover of my soul is here!

*You become **my delicious feast** even when **my enemies dare to fight**. You **anoint me** with the fragrance of your Holy Spirit; you give me all I can drink of you until **my heart overflows**. So why would I fear the future?*

Psalms 23:5 TPT

God makes sure all of my needs are met and even gives me more than I can possibly need so that I can share with my enemies. My enemies begin to see the overflow of love that only the good Shepherd can provide. By inviting my enemies to the feast, they become my friends and we continue on with the future that God has in store for all who eat from His table. By feasting on God, we never hunger or thirst again!

*For your **goodness and love pursue me all the days of my life**. Then afterward, when my life is through, I'll return to your glorious presence to be **forever with you!***"

Psalms 23:6 TPT

Making the daily decision to surrender my will over to God guarantees me love for eternity. I remain in God's presence and under His protection forever! I had searched my entire life for a love that was right here all along. Not only am I experiencing heaven right here on Earth, I get to do the same thing with God for eternity.

Revelation Moment

On my best day, I could not defeat the enemy in my own strength, I could not defeat religion, death, poverty, sickness, I could not defeat anything. Because I understand that God created me, I have assumed the position of surrender so I could become the superhero of my life because my Daddy is the ultimate superhero. God will put us in places that we never asked for, but those places are a part of God's plan for our life. The things that I went through wasn't meant to keep me bound, but they were purposed so God could get the glory out of my life. God allowed me to go through so I could get through and be an example for others to follow.

Many people think the posture of surrender means that you are giving up, in fact the enemy will try to convince you that you're giving up. But if you assume the position of surrender, you begin to realize that the very things that you thought were important are only scratching the surface of what God has planned for your life. If you remain in a posture of surrender when those distractions, temptations, delays, desires, and attacks come; you will know that God's got it so you don't need to worry about it.

I realize that living for God in such a sinful world can be very challenging, but I can assure you that God is faithful! If we spent more time in the Word of God and less time watching TV or doing the things of the world, we will be surprised how God will blow your mind. We are influenced by our surroundings. Let's start surrounding ourselves with God, the good Shepherd and the people (sheep) of God! So when we have problems, we don't get the world's solutions, we get solutions that last forever because they are from our Creator! Allow God to order your steps. Learn the lesson so you can lessen the pain. Allow God to shape and mold you into HIS image the 1st time so you He doesn't have to keep starting over.

Repentance is daily surrender to God's will and not our own. Remaining in a posture of surrender, allows us to avoid all extremes and the plan of the enemy to dilute our minds. When I made the decision to completely surrender to God, I realized that this is the pathway to true freedom that has put me on roads that have exceeded my wildest dreams (Ephesians 3:20). Assuming the position of surrender at all times has taken me from glory to glory to a better than blessed life!

"God will reverse the curse when you surrender."

–Tuwana Nicole

Chapter 19

Jesus will Reverse the Curse

Once you were dead because of your disobedience and your many sins. You used to live in sin, just like the rest of the world, obeying the devil—the commander of the powers in the unseen world. He is the spirit at work in the hearts of those who refuse to obey God. All of us used to live that way, following the passionate desires and inclinations of our sinful nature.

Ephesians 2:1-3a NLT

The enemy's plan was to teach me how to depend on myself and become the god of my own life. But God's plan was to teach me how to stay at the feet of Jesus so I would not only know His voice, but obey His voice. God uses our circumstances to bring us to a place of obedience to Him.

All of us took the curses that had been passed down to us, not knowing that we had taken on the sins of our ancestors. Because we were born into a fallen world that is run by the enemy, our fate was already sealed if Satan had the final word. By generations of our families conforming to the ways of the world, it is only possible to renew our minds and escape the plan of the enemy by not only accepting Jesus to be our personal Savior, but also the Lord of our lives. Then by fully trusting Him to lead and guide our lives, we can reverse the curse unfruitfulness in our lives by becoming generational curse breakers for our family.

The Party is Over, Now What?

The devil is hiding behind the very things that we think are ok. He has perverted the things that God meant for good and is making them evil. Everyone likes to enjoy being around family and friends, getting married, taking vacations, and going out to eat. Jesus' first miracle was when He turned water into wine at a wedding (John 2:1-11).

What do we do after the party? What do we do after the vacation, after the newness of the relationship wears off, after all the money's gone, when the kids grow up? We still have to deal with our life. Many parties bring out our bad behavior. We get drunk, be promiscuous, and spend too much, say things that we shouldn't, or simply act a fool. All these are a cry for help. If we continue to seek the party, this becomes our way of life. After the party is over, we go back to our miserable lives that we needed to escape from in the first place.

The way of the world always starts out fun and exciting, but after a while we end up used and hurt. The devil makes things look good, but once we go deeper we find out that we've been drinking poison! Just because we can doesn't mean that we should! God is the one who picks us up after the world has used us up so remember that the next time you want to choose the world's way!

If the body of Christ is functioning the way God intended, we would be willing to encourage our brothers and sisters who are in the throes of sin. When we're truly free, we want to help as many people as we can get free too! If we see something, we say something! Many people saw me struggle and said nothing because they had allowed the enemy to silence them into being a satisfied pew sitter instead of a sanctified go-getter! When I began to realize that no matter how many vacations I took, no matter how many guys I met, no matter how many businesses I started; at the end of the day I was still depressed and lonely. God has made me the answer to my own prayers for others who are lost. Our life experiences always point us back to God.

Generational Curse Breaker

Isn't it obvious that God deliberately chose men and women that the culture overlooks and exploits and abuses, chose these "nobodies" to expose the hollow presentations of the "somebodies"?

1 Corinthians 1:27-28 MSG

God takes the foolish things of the world to show Himself mighty and strong. I struggled so much that I couldn't see the light at the end of the tunnel. God reassured me just like He did Gideon (Judges 6:15-16) that He would be with me and I would overcome the plan of the enemy. God allowed me to be lost so I could be found by Him. God showed me that I was royalty and that He was making me the answer to my prayers. I didn't understand how I was the One that God wanted to use me to break the curse in my family. I was always asking God questions that He had been revealing to me since I was a baby. God meant for me to be rejected, an outcast, set apart, ostracized, overlooked, under estimated, thrown away, and different. God allowed me to go through many fires so I could come out refined just like that beautiful butterfly that has gone the process of dying to self so God can get the glory!

Flashlight vs. Lighthouse

"Then Jesus said, "I am light to the world and those who embrace me will experience life-giving light, and they will never walk in darkness."

John 8:12 TPT

When there is darkness, we cannot see or navigate properly. We bump into things that hurt us, we bump into others and hurt them. We are basically walking zombies. We have the appearance of being alive, but because we're in the dark we are dead. Oftentimes we will pick up flashlights in an effort to see more clearly. A flashlight represents anything that we pick up in our desperation, instead picking up God. The flashlight could be religion, which only gives us a small view of how to get to the light. The flashlight could be going to school, which will only give us knowledge that leads us to prosper in this world's system. Because the flashlight has a limited range, we still have a limited view. So we still can't see everything clearly. We soon realize that the light is too dim because we continue to repeat the same things that we did before. We keep bumping into things, and bumping into others, we realize that the little light we have still doesn't give us what we need to see everything clearly. A flashlight provides just enough light to see what's right in front of us, but not enough to light to illuminate our surroundings. Flashlights show up in our lives having the appearance of God, but when you look more closely, you see its still Satan trying to keep us blinded.

*"But everything exposed by the light becomes visible-
and everything that is illuminated becomes a light.
This is why it is said: "Wake up sleeper, rise from the
dead and Christ will shine on you."*

Ephesians 5:13-14 NIV

I don't want to be just another flashlight in the world. I
want my life to shine so bright that others want to
know more about Jesus Christ. Jesus is the life light.
Being in relationship with him allows us to also become
lighthouses for others to follow as we lead them to him.
A lighthouse illuminates everything around it and
serves as a navigational tool to lead others to safety.
When we embrace Jesus, we can expose the darkness
around us and bring others safely into the boat of life.
Because we have allowed Jesus to be our life light, we
become carriers of His light everywhere we go. We
become a lighthouse that leads others out of
darkness. We become lighthouses in a world full of
flashlights.

Revelation Moment

*"This is the life-giving message we heard him share and
it's still ringing in our ears. We now repeat his words to
you: God is pure light. You will never find even a trace
of darkness in him. If we claim that we share life with
him, but keep walking in the realm of darkness, we're
fooling ourselves and not living the truth. But if we
keep living in the pure light that surrounds him, we
share unbroken fellowship with one another, and the
blood of Jesus, his Son continually cleanses us from all
sin."*

1 John 1:5-7 TPT

From Rejected to Redeemed

As I began to accept God's life giving message, I began to understand that God meant for me to be different, from my birth to the abuse, not fitting in with my family or anywhere I went. God meant for me to be rejected so he could redeem me for my good and His glory. I spent the first 33 years of my life trying to fit in, then for the last 11 years I have been allowing God to shape and mold me into who He purposed for me to be. God wants me to walk in the light so I could become a light for others.

Since the enemy knew the plan God had for my life. He used my fear of rejection, disappointments, and failures to continue to wreak havoc in my life. Having struggled for many years of trying to fight the enemy in my own strength, I started learning how to fight in prayer. I began to put on the full armor of God so I could overcome the plan of the enemy.

Sometimes we give more energy to people and situations (bad relationships, jobs, and obtaining material possessions) that are simply not worth it, yet we don't give enough energy to the people and situations (God, children, family, setting a good example, doing what's right) that are more than worth it. I thank God for giving me the courage and strength to say goodbye to my worldly values so I can walk into my better than blessed life!

I finally saw the opportunity to reverse the curse in my family. I didn't know how God was going to do it, but because God said it that settled it for me. I began to rest at the feet of Jesus instead of fighting the world in my own strength. I had been fighting for so long and I was tired of fighting.

Even though I had previously made the decision to accept Jesus as my Savior, now I began to understand the importance of allowing Jesus to be the Lord of my life. Only through the continual surrendering of my will to God and believing His plan for my life will it become possible for me to become the generational curse breaker. By allowing metamorphosis to take place in my life, my obedience to the process has brought me to levels in God I never thought was possible.

Jesus says, "All things are possible for the one who believes and trusts [in Me]!"

Mark 9:23b AMP

Not only do I believe, I will trust and obey God!!

Are you going to stay enslaved or are you going to seek true freedom that it is only found in a relationship with Jesus Christ? Don't continue to pay for what you want, yet beg for what you need. It's time to allow Jesus to reverse the curse the curse of darkness off your family line.

"Don't live life in hindsight, live with insight."

-Tuvana Nicole

Chapter 20

Love

O God of my life, I'm lovesick for you in this weary wilderness. I thirst with the deepest longings to love you more, with cravings in my heart that can't be described. Such yearning grips my soul for you, my God! I'm energized every time I enter your heavenly sanctuary to seek more of your power and drink in more of your glory. For your tender mercies mean more to me than life itself. How I love and praise you, God! Daily I will worship you passionately and with all my heart. My arms will wave to you like banners of praise. I overflow with praise when I come before you, for the anointing of your presence satisfies me like nothing else. You are such a rich banquet of pleasure to my soul. I lie awake each night thinking of you and reflecting on how you help me like a father. I sing through the night under your splendor-shadow, offering up to you my songs of delight and joy! With passion I pursue and cling to you. Because I feel your grip on my life, I keep my soul close to your heart.

Psalms 63:1-9 TPT

Now that I am developing a deeper, more intimate relationship with God I couldn't possibly view loving Him as merely a commandment (Mark 12:30). I consider it an honor and a privilege to be known and loved by God. It was finally sinking in what

From Rejected to Redeemed

Jesus meant when He told me that He was the ONE that I had been searching for my entire life. I thought I understood before, but now I truly understand that nothing or no one could ever take the place of God. Everything that I was missing, I found it in God.

Who wouldn't love a God that leads us to everything that is for our good and for His glory? I always wanted to know what love was. After searching high and low for many years, I finally have the lover of my soul. I wouldn't trade this love for anything that this world has to offer. I never thought I would ever know what love is. Every time I think I understand the depths of God's love, I realize that I'm only getting a taste of who God is. God is in essence love. It took me a little longer to finally see, but now that I have tasted and seen it up close and personal, I'm never letting go!

Love Self & Love Others

And the second is this: 'You must love your neighbor in the same way you love yourself.' You will never find a greater commandment than these.

Mark 12:31 TPT

There is no way that you can effectively love your neighbor if you do not love yourself. The only way that you can love yourself is if you allow God to teach you what love is. Because I had never experienced love like this before, I found myself falling back into my old ways of what I thought love was. Situation after situation, I kept getting hurt. I began to realize that God is the only one that can show me how to love like He does. God began to show me that even though I didn't love myself, I did know how to love others. God showed me that I had always treated people the way that I wanted to be treated (Matthew 7:12).

From Rejected to Redeemed

I wasn't perfect in it, but I always had a high regard for how I interacted with others. In fact, God showed me that my ability to look past other people's faults and to see their needs was a gift from Him.

Guard Your Heart

So above all, guard the affections of your heart, for they affect all that you are. Pay attention to the welfare of your innermost being, for from there flows the wellspring of life.

Proverbs 4:23 TPT

God began to show me that I needed to guard my heart because even though I was loving my neighbor as myself, the enemy was using my lack of self-love to cause me to become bitter and resentful for not having the love reciprocated. For many, many years of my life and even after initially accepting Jesus Christ to be my redeemer, I still struggled with this. I was so gullible and believed everything that people told me. I always believed the best of everyone that I met.

I found myself being deceived and manipulated on a regular basis until one day after dating a pastor who was dating me and several other women at the same time. My mind was still diluted by my desire to marry a pastor so I could fulfill God's purpose for my life. I was yet to overcome the lust of the flesh. The Holy Spirit began to tell me to guard my heart. I kept asking, how do I guard my heart Lord? God led me back to Proverbs 4 again.

I'd spent so much of my life giving people the benefit of the doubt, always believing the best, looking for the best in them, and being a true friend that I didn't know how to shift my mindset. Still unsure of how to move forward, I continued to ask God how do I guard my heart. God, "you told me to love like you love, yet I'm still struggling."

This gift that you have placed within me is causing me to die inside. This gift has made it impossible for me to hate people even when I want to. So how can I guard my heart? God led me to this scripture:

"Don't waste what is holy on people who are unholy. Don't throw your pearls to pigs! They will trample the pearls, then turn and attack you."

Matthew 7:6 NLT

Now it is becoming clearer how the enemy will use anyone to thwart the plans of God. Only someone who is living for the devil would want to treat someone who is treating them well this poorly. I still haven't quite mastered guarding my heart, but God has been showing me how to become persistent in my prayers for those that choose to treat me poorly in spite of how well I may treat them. By remaining prayerful, I have been able to guard my heart and now I no longer fall prey to the people that the enemy works through to attempt to make me shift my focus away from love.

My relationship with God is allowing me to come to the realization that no matter how much I love someone, I cannot make them love me back. Love cannot be forced. No matter how great of a friend that I am to some people, they may never have the capacity to be a good friend to me.

Through the leading of the Holy Spirit, I have been able to keep moving forward despite what people think about me or how they treat me. I have finally been able to release the pain of my past, present, and future by continuing to love others like God loves me! God showed me that the best way I can show my love for others even if they are no longer a part of my life is to pray for them. Prayer is the greatest act of love, especially when it's someone that has done harm to you.

Love Gives and Forgives

So don't be shocked, beloved brothers and sisters, if you experience the world's hatred. Yet we can be assured that we have been translated from spiritual death into spiritual life because we love the family of believers. A loveless life remains spiritually dead. Everyone who keeps hating a fellow believer is a murderer, and you know that no murderer has eternal life residing in him. This is how we have discovered love's reality: Jesus sacrificed his life for us. Because of this great love, we should be willing to lay down our lives for one another. If anyone sees a fellow believer in need and has the means to help him, yet shows no pity and closes his heart against him, how is it even possible that God's love lives in him? Beloved children, our love can't be an abstract theory we only talk about, but a way of life demonstrated through our loving deeds. We know that the truth lives within us because we demonstrate love in action, which will reassure our hearts in his presence.

1 John 3:13-19 TPT

One of the hardest acts of love that really taught me what God's love is all about was when I made the decision to forgive the man who murdered my mother. It was very difficult in the beginning, but I soon remembered how God had forgiven me even though I was undeserving of His forgiveness (Romans 5:8). Some may call it grace, others may call it mercy, even forgiveness; but God has shown me that it is called LOVE! All the attributes of God point to love. So if we are truly in Him, there is no way we won't love everyone, even those who don't understand what love is.

Love always brings out the best in us. Fake love only gives us what we want. God wouldn't be a good Father if He always does everything we want Him to do. God teaches us how to live a life of service and sacrifice to others. God teaches us how to love those who do not love us. Real love must be lived out loud, not just talked about.

"Love is patient, love is kind. It does not envy, it does not boast, it is not proud. It does not dishonor others, it is not self-seeking, it is not easily angered, it keeps no record of wrongs. Love does not delight in evil but rejoices with the truth. It always protects, always trusts, always hopes, always perseveres. Love never fails. But where there are prophecies, they will cease; where there are tongues, they will be stilled; where there is knowledge, it will pass away."

1 Corinthians 13:4-8 NIV

There was a young lady that was in our homeless shelter that I had to dismiss from the program because of her disregard of the rules and blatant disrespect for others in the program. About 2 years after she was dismissed, she shows up at the door to let me know that I was the truth. She went on to say that I was real, I was love. She just wanted to stop by and make amends for the problems that she had caused when she was in our program.

Everyone can't have and doesn't deserve a front row seat to our life! But love should always be the answer when they show up at our door. Real love is demonstrated. It will challenge you, make you grow, make you better. Even though this young lady didn't appreciate our program when she was in it, she soon learned that it was the best thing that had happened to her. I'm so thankful that she was able to see the error of her ways and I was able to answer the door of love so she could receive restoration.

Revelation Moment

But the love of God will be perfected within the one who obeys God's Word. We can be sure that we've truly come to living in intimacy with God, not just by saying, "I am intimate with God," but by walking in the footsteps of Jesus.

1 John 2:5-6 TPT

Now that I have insight, I no longer have to live with hindsight. Since God is love, love should be the motivating factor to everything that I do. Nothing that I do will be successful if it's not done with love. So God has given me more clarity on how to live a life of love by seeking to love like He does. My love must always be pure and sincere with Jesus being my example. Jesus reminded me of Him going to cross to reconcile me back to God. He reminded me of the difficulty He had carrying my burdens to the cross. Jesus not only carried my burdens to the cross, love kept Him on the cross. Jesus reminded me that by choosing to take up my cross, I will learn how to love like He does. The more I keep my focus on Jesus and remember the perfect work that He did on the cross makes me experience love like I never thought possible.

But Christ proved God's passionate love for us by dying in our place while we were still lost and ungodly!

Romans 5:8 TPT

When we willfully choose to do what God asks even when we don't want to do it is obedience. As I continue to allow God to have complete control of my life, I am learning how to live without fear and love without limits. This love causes me to want to seek more unity in the body of Christ. This love compels me to seek the good of others above myself. This love has caused a prayer warrior to arise in me like never before. Everything that the enemy meant for evil, God has turned it around for my good and His glory all because I took the limits off my limited idea of what love is and allowed the lover of my soul to lead the way!

"Your actions are a direct reflection of what you believe."

−Tuwana Nicole

Part 4

Living a Better than Blessed Life

Better Than Blessed is defined as having joy in spite of your circumstances while embodying the courage and the strength to do and be the impossible because of your relationship with God.

You will be blessed more than any other people.

Deuteronomy 7:14a NIV

I pray that the light of God will illuminate the eyes of your imagination, flooding you with light, until you experience the full revelation of the hope of his calling-that is, the wealth of God's glorious inheritances that he finds in us, his holy ones! I pray that you will continually experience the immeasurable greatness of God's power made available to you through faith. Then your lives will be an advertisement of this immense power as it works through you! This is the mighty power that was released when God raised Christ from the dead and exalted him to the place of highest honor and supreme authority in the heavenly realm! And now he is exalted as first above every ruler, authority, government, and realm of power in existence! He is gloriously enthroned over every name that is ever praised, not only in this age, but in the age that is coming! And he alone is the leader and source of everything needed in the church. God has put everything beneath the authority of Jesus Christ and has given him the highest rank above all others. And now we, his church are his body on earth that which fills him is being filled by it!

Ephesians 1:18-23 TPT

Chapter 21

God's Mysteries Revealed

*Then Jesus exclaimed, "Father, thank you, for you are Lord, the Supreme Ruler over heaven and earth! And **you have hidden the great revelation of your authority from those who are proud and wise in their own eyes.** Instead, **you have shared it with these who humble themselves.** Yes, Father, your plan delights your heart, as you've chosen this way to extend your kingdom— **by giving it to those who have become like trusting children.** You have entrusted me with all that you are and all that you have. No one fully and intimately knows the Son except the Father. And no one fully and intimately knows the Father except the Son. But the Son is able to unveil the Father to anyone he chooses.*

Matthew 11:25-27 TPT

People always say that God is a mysterious God, but the more that I walk with Him I realize that God is only mysterious to those who don't know Him and are not willing to go through the process.. In every stage of my life, since accepting Jesus to be my personal Lord and Savior, I have had a personal encounter with God. When I was 13, God showed me that I was the generational curse breaker in my family. He also showed me that I was looking for love in all the wrong places. When I found myself at the feet of Jesus at the age of 33, He showed me the same things. But this time He began to show me how much He loved me and I was His messenger of the Good News and Royalty. Around age 37, He began to show me that He was going to expand my territory. He had me to start different businesses. At age 42, God began to show me that He was making me the answer to other people's prayers. The more intimately we know God, the more He reveals Himself to us.

*He explained, "You've been given the intimate experience of insight into the hidden truths and mysteries of the realm of heaven's kingdom, but they have not. For everyone **who listens with an open heart will receive progressively more revelation** until he has more than enough. But those who don't listen with an open, teachable heart, even the understanding that they think they have will be taken from them."*

Matthew 13:11-12 TPT

God revealed His mysteries to me so I could understand that there was a purpose in my pain and that my ultimate life mission was to reveal His mysteries to the least of these. I needed to learn how to handle rejection so that I could be able to stand with boldness and proclaim what thus says the Lord. He wanted me to overcome rejection so I could become comfortable in my own skin. God allowed me to be rejected so I would learn how to trust Him and trust Him ONLY! Who would have thought it was this simple to come into the knowledge of who God is? I know I didn't know that when Jesus kept knocking on the door of my heart (Revelation 3:20). God was drawing me to Him, all while the enemy was luring me in. Satan is the master deceiver which is totally opposite of God, the Master Revealer.

Servant of God

Your attitude should be the same as that of Christ Jesus: who, being in the very nature of God, did not consider equality with God something to be grasped, but made himself nothing, taking the very nature of a servant, being made in human likeness. And being found in appearance as a man, he humbled himself and became obedient to death- even death on the cross!

Philippians 2:5-8

I didn't understand why God told me to always call myself a servant of God when I surrendered my life to Him in 2008. Even though I didn't understand, I obeyed the voice of the Lord. It brought me some ridicule even from those in the church. Many asked me, "why do you call yourself a servant?" I would answer them with Matthew 23:11-12 which states, "The greatest among you must be a servant. But those who exalt themselves will be humbled, and those who humble themselves will be exalted." Even when I would give this answer, I still hadn't been able to completely wrap my head around it. Iin our world system, we are called CEO's, Presidents, Managers, Managing Partners, Supervisors, and the like. We seek those positions because in the world's system, those titles bring us power and authority.
As I continue to grow in my relationship with God, everything that He has ever told me is beginning to make perfect sense now. A servant doesn't seek His own good. He does what his Master tells him to do. A servant seeks the good of others, not himself. That philosophy goes directly against our world value

system. Jesus said that He came to serve and not be served (Matthew 20:28), yet many in the body of Christ want just that: to be served! Many want the titles, the accolades, and even the platform. We seek the gifts of the Holy Spirit without the Fruit of the Holy Spirit. I'm learning that all of those things automatically come when we remain true to the heart of who God called us to be. Jesus Christ was a servant and the perfect example, we must take that same posture as our model for life. Once we're able to completely place our identity in Christ, we understand that a Servant of God is the highest position we can have in the Kingdom of God no matter what our gifts are. Let's walk like Jesus did.

Kingdom Business

The Holy Spirit began to lead me back to the beatitudes, which mean blessedness. God wanted to show me the correlation between the ministry name and the business name that He had given me: To God Be the Glory Ministries & Better Than Blessed Enterprises. God wanted me to merge the ministry with the marketplace to make it a marketplace ministry.

God wanted me to see that everything that He is leading us to do is for our good, but it is ultimately for His glory. The business is always His business. We're in this world, but not of this world. We are to develop a Kingdom Mindset, not a worldly mindset. It is meant to draw people to Him, not ourselves. I pray that you will receive the same revelation from these scriptures like I did:

Blessed are the poor in spirit: (at the end of your rope, those who recognize their need for God, outcasts, rejects, mistreated, overlooked, abused) for theirs is the kingdom of heaven. Blessed are they that mourn: (when you feel like all is lost, you will never be loved, you will never be appreciated, your life is over, repenting of your sins) for they shall be comforted. Blessed are the meek: (when you are ok with the little that you have, when you give to others, are good to others) for they shall inherit the earth. Blessed are they which do hunger and thirst after righteousness: (you want to do what God requires of you, you are desperate for whatever God wants to do in your life, you want to be in right standing with God, when you only want God, you know that only God can satisfy the deepest longings of your soul) for they shall be filled. Blessed are the merciful: (you care for everyone, you love everyone, you are forgiving) for they shall obtain mercy. Blessed are the pure in heart: (you have integrity, moral courage, Godly character, you treat people the way you want to be treated) for they shall see God. Blessed are the peacemakers: (you seek the good of everyone, you want people to get along, you seek unity) for they shall be called the children of God. Blessed are they which are persecuted for righteousness' sake: (you do what's right no matter what others do and when no one is watching, people hate you because you do what is right) for theirs is the kingdom of heaven. Blessed are ye, when men shall revile you, and persecute you, and shall say all manner of evil against you falsely, for my sake. Rejoice, and be exceeding glad: for great is your reward in heaven for so persecuted they the prophets which were before you.

Matthew 5:3-12 KJV

I thought I understood why God had me starting certain types of businesses. God continues to unveil His plans for my life and reveal things that were still a mystery. I now realize that ultimately everything that He has led me to do is to bring glory to His name, not to necessarily bring money to my pockets, nor to build an earthly empire and attempt to bring glory to His name through it. God's Kingdom is not of this world, so the only reason He gives us success is to show Himself strong when we are weak (2 Corinthians 12:10). Matthew 6:33 explains, *but seek ye first the kingdom of God and his righteousness, and all these things shall be added unto you.*
God has made me the head and not the tail, the lender and not the borrower, above and not beneath, to be an example for others to follow Him and only Him. But we must understand that obtaining wealth and success is not the prize. God is the prize!

Revelation Moment

God has now revealed to us his mysterious will regarding Christ—which is to fulfill his own good plan. And this is the plan: At the right time he will bring everything together under the authority of Christ— everything in heaven and on earth.

Ephesians 1:9-10 NLT
I literally cried as I wrote this chapter because God was still revealing more of His plans to me. God is constantly stretching my faith and refining me more into His image. If we're making all the decisions in our lives or looking to the world for answers, where does God come in (1 John 4:4-6)? God's wisdom opens up God's mysteries. Now I see why I always had an issue with denominationalism/religion. It truly is a tool of the enemy that keeps us bound. I truly understand how we

can perish from lack of knowledge and how the curses continue from generation to generation
(Read Hosea 4).

God is the Alpha & Omega, the beginning and the end. God operates in and out of time to allow our life experiences to point us closer to Him. God is measuring us through His Word, The Holy Bible. We have everything that our Daddy has. He is our peace. We have to trust God to be our source. We don't have to make anything happen. We simply recognize that it has already happened. All we have to do is properly position ourselves through prayer, actively listening, and obedience to God. Then our faith will begin to defy the world's logic. Our lives may remain a mystery to others, but we will experience the fullness of God realizing that our biggest revelations from God may never change this world, but they should be ever changing our world! As *Colossians 1:13 NLT states, For he has rescued us from the kingdom of darkness and transferred us into the Kingdom of his dear Son.*

"God reveals His mysteries to those who are in relationship with Him."

–Tuwana Nicole

Chapter 22

Living Testimony

Our people defeated Satan because of the blood of the Lamb and the message of God. They were willing to give up their lives.

Revelation 12:11 CEVUK

We defeat the enemy because of the finished work of Jesus on the Cross and giving our testimony of the transforming work that God has done and is doing in our lives. Then we continue to allow Jesus to perfect our faith (Hebrews 12:2). I am a living, breathing, walking testament of the goodness of God. I am a living epistle, a living testimony. After I found myself at the feet of Jesus over eleven years ago, that encounter has changed the entire trajectory of my life. God wants to get the glory out of our lives. I'm not sinless, but I sin less because I want to see the glory of God in my life. I want to be the change in the world that I want to see. I want to break generational curses, see blind eyes open, I want to see the deaf hear, and I want to see the lame walk. I make the decision every day to die to self so I can have a testimony about the goodness of the Lord.

Money Is Not the Goal

"Without the help of the LORD it is useless to build a home or to guard a city. It is useless to get up early and stay up late in order to earn a living. God takes care of his own, even while they sleep."

Psalms 127:1-2 CEVUK

When God led me to Deuteronomy 7, I really thought that He was going to bless me only with earthly riches, but I soon learned that He was blessing me with Himself! God is faithful to His promises. But I'm learning that there's always a deeper revelation to God's promises. The goal is for us to make room to not only host Him, but God wants to dwell within us. God wants to build us up into a home that is tailor made just for Him to live in. God wants us to be a mighty fortress, strong tower, and lighthouse where He is the life light!

Because we seek God and God alone, He always makes sure that we are taken care of. He says He will take care of us even while we sleep. That's why He invites us into His rest. If we continue to abide in Him and seek His face, we will automatically get His hand. So instead of looking for RESOURCES, go straight to the SOURCE! As long as we continue to seek God, He will make us shine like heaven on Earth. When God inhabits your life, blessings never run out because we have made our lives the place where God resides! It's very important to seek the heart of God, then we will automatically receive the hand of God.

Get Wisdom

Wisdom and money can get you almost anything, but only wisdom can save your life.

Ecclesiastes 7:12

I remember at one point in my life, I was always overwhelmed and unhappy. Now the things that once bothered me don't bother me anymore. The things that once made me depressed, don't make me depressed anymore. The things that used to break me, don't break me anymore. God is continuing to give me everything that I need to deal with the cares of life. I am a living testimony because I asked God to give me wisdom.

As I continue to delight myself in the Lord through the surrendering of my will to God's will, my thoughts became like His thoughts, my ways become His ways. My desires became like God's desires. I'm reminded of King Solomon who asked God for wisdom. God not only gave him wisdom, but gave him riches too. God has done it for me too! Wisdom is the key to life. Wisdom has saved my life, money has simply sweetened the deal!!

God is the Reward

And the King will answer them, "Don't you know? When you cared for one of the least important of these my little ones, my true brothers and sisters, you demonstrated love for me,"

Matthew 25:40 TPT

From Rejected to Redeemed

When God led me to start a homeless shelter, I knew that He wanted me to serve others. In the beginning, I wanted to feel like I was contributing to the world and making an impact. I wanted to have a sense of dignity, but God was showing me that I still needed deliverance from self. God called me to this ministry, but a part of me thought that I would finally get love and acceptance by helping others. I was in for a rude awakening. Just like so many others that go into ministry thinking that the reward of ministry would bring them love. I learned within a few years that God is the reward, who is the essence of real love.

God may want us to have a homeless shelter, church, business, outreach; but at the end of the day, the purpose is to draw us closer to Him, to bring glory to His name, and to assist anyone who is without Him whether they are physically homeless or spiritually homeless. If what we do in the name of the Lord is to draw people to ourselves or bring a missing piece to our lives, the devil will attempt to dismantle it. We know by seeing other ministries in the past just how easy it is to destroy what was originally meant for good. We must make sure that our goal is to get them to HIM, who is the source of everything. Then God will be our reward.

Revelation Moment

Empty out of my heart everything that is false-every lie, and every crooked thing. And give me neither undue poverty nor undue wealth-but rather feed my soul with the measure of prosperity that pleases you.

Proverbs 30:8 TPT

This better than blessed life defies the world's logic. This better than blessed life goes against our cultural values. When God first revealed to me the term "better than blessed" around 2009, I didn't quite understand what it meant. At this point I had only been walking with God for about a year. Then In 2016, the Holy Spirit told me to start an enterprise and name it Better Than Blessed Enterprises. I still didn't understand completely why He told me to do this, but chose to be obedient.

When our true values align with God's word, we begin to understand our purpose. We don't need to feel validated by how we look, what we have, or how we perform for people. God's approval is more than enough! Because of my obedience to God, I have seen heaven come to Earth in my own personal life. I have seen God move supernaturally through my life circumstances. As a descendant of Abraham through the redeeming blood of Jesus, God has kept His promises to me.

Blessed is she who has believed that the Lord would fulfill his promises to her!

Luke 1:45 NIV

From Rejected to Redeemed

Here are some of the promises that God has fulfilled to make me a living testimony:

1. **Blind Eyes Opened-**God used my physical limitation of wearing glasses since the age of 5 to show himself mighty in my life. When I made the decision to continue pursuing God's plan for my life, my vision began becoming clearer and clearer. Not only has God restored my physical vision to 20/20, He is giving me 20/20 vision in the spiritual realm.
2. **Deaf Ears Unstopped-**God took what the enemy tried to use to make me think was a mental illness and has made it clear that I hear from God and have been hearing from Him all along. God has given me many prophetic assignments to be His voice in these perilous times. Every prophecy that He has given me has come to pass or it has brought repentance.
3. **Healed to Healer** God has restored my health completely helping me to lose over 100 lbs and given me a ministry to bring physical & spiritual healing others. My testimony has inspired others to believe in the healing power of Jesus.
4. **Delivered to Deliverer-**God has made me the answer to many people's cries to Him. He has enabled me to help others not be deceived by the enemy and those he uses through the writing of books to doing workshops, speaking engagements, and retreats.
5. **Confused to Counselor-**God used my constant state of confusion and have given me clarity on who He is and has revealed many of His mysteries to me so that I can help others gain clarity and give them a clear path that leads to Him.

6. **Wanderer to Traveler With A Purpose**-God took my desire to travel to escape my life and He has turned it into a business that put me on the path to becoming debt-free. He also uses my travels as a platform to travel the world for His purpose and to bring others back to life! Now I no longer have to escape life because my life is surrendered to Christ!

7. **Better Than Blessed**-God has positioned me to be debt free through different business deals that I entered into at His direction and the ability to purchase properties where we are the lender and not the borrower. God has truly made me more blessed than I ever imagined despite all of the impossibilities that I was facing.

Since I have allowed my life to become an altar for God, He is ever refining, shaping, and molding me more into the image of Jesus Christ. My life is becoming a scripture that others will read and be encouraged to become living epistle for generations to come. So when people read the story of our lives, they won't simply think that God is still a MYSTERY that only worked that way in Biblical times. Many will see that God is still the same God yesterday, today, and forever. By becoming living testimonies, prayerfully everyone I encounter will want to know more about God and His Plan so they can overcome the plan of the enemy rewriting HIS-story!

"Revelation always proceeds transformation."

-Tuwana Nicole

Chapter 23

Endure the Rain to Reign

*For you know that when your faith is tested,
your endurance has a chance to grow.*

James 1:3 NLT

Many times we would rather escape and avoid reality, but God wants us to embrace it. When we embrace God's plan, we are empowered to overcome anything that comes our way. I have gone through many trials and tribulations to become the living testimony that I am today. Matthew 11:12 tells us the Kingdom of God is going to continue to suffer violence. So we must be prepared for the enemy to bring out all the big guns to stop everything that we do for God. Know that he will stop at nothing to see us fail. When we made the decision to shift, turn, repent, and press more into God; The enemy fights us for every inch of territory that we are gaining for the Kingdom of God. At the end of the day, we understand that is his job so we must keep our gaze on Jesus and don't lose focus and get out of character.

On the brink of a breakthrough is when the enemy fights us the hardest. He doesn't want us to acquire the knowledge that only God can give. He doesn't want us to go to the next level in God. Writing this book was very, very difficult for me. Everything that could possibly go wrong, went wrong. I had issues with every phase of this book. My book manuscript was deleted from my computer, the book cover has been wrong with every sample printed, having issues with getting the book printed on time, and having to reschedule many other projects due to delays. I didn't expect to get everything done at the absolute last minute, but nonetheless I knew I was going to have lots and lots of opposition. The enemy wanted me to believe that I am losing when in essence, I definitely know that I'm winning. In fact, I have already won because of the sacrifice that Jesus made on the cross. God has brought me too far to leave me now. Anything we do for the glory of God will be attacked. The enemy doesn't want us to believe that God can use us. He knows that when we believe, he is in trouble.

Everyone Can't Handle the Truth

Jesus said to the people who believed in him, "You are truly my disciples if you remain faithful to my teachings. And you will know the truth, and the truth will set you free."

John 6:31-32 NLT

People love you until you tell them the truth. Keep telling the truth anyway! I remember one of my mentors told me that the closer that I walk with God, the fewer and fewer people would be on the journey with me. I have definitely found that to be very true. Especially when it comes to the basic desires of this world. Most Christians are fine with not physically committing murder or stealing from someone, but we murder people with our words, we withhold help when it's needed. We don't keep our word. We manipulate, we lie, we cheat, and we steal from each other on a daily basis.

We don't even mind sharing our love for God with others until we begin to feel the sting of persecution. We tell everyone oh how we love Jesus until all your friends walk away because they believe we're taking this Jesus thing too far and we're left to stand alone. Or when our faith requires us to tell a customer the truth, but telling the truth may get us fired from our job because it goes against company policy. What about having to admit that you struggle with being faithful to one person? Can you be transparent enough to tell the truth even if it means that it could damage your relationship?

Telling the truth is the reason why Jesus was crucified. The very people that God sent Him to save, rejected Him. So it is very clear why I have been rejected my entire life. When people are not ready to live a life of truth and want to continue to hide behind masks, they hate those who tell them the truth. I used to wonder why I was so hated by people. Because most people want to continue to pretend and hang around people who will condone their mess, they tend to avoid people who will call them out on their mess. People who don't desire to grow and be challenged, they avoid me. They have a tendency to only want to come around when they need something.

Have I really become your enemy because I tell you the truth?

Galatians 4:16 TPT

The devil is the main one who not only hates the truth, he can't handle the truth. The enemy hates to be called a liar. If we want to disarm him. Simply call him a liar and watch him flee (James 4:7). Since recognizing that he absolutely hates it, I tried it. At first the devil tried to turn and make it seem like I was the liar, but when I stood my ground, he would get away from me. In the past, the devil would use this tactic and it would make me shrink back because I didn't want to be rejected. But now I have overcome that devil and I know his tricks and not I'm falling for it anymore.

My Mother, The Martyr

I never forget many Christians coming up to me after my Mother was murdered asking, "why did your Mother help that family?" or "Why did she let him in knowing that he was on drugs?" At the time, I didn't have an answer. I just remember feeling hurt that they would even ask me that, especially since they were older Christians who should have been more seasoned in the Word of God. Even though I didn't have an intimate relationship with God at that time, I knew that her death could not have been in vain. I felt like they were already dishonoring her memory by implying that she was responsible for her own death by putting herself in a position that shows the love of God.

My mother was not perfect, however I saw God move mightily in her life. My friends used to tease me about my Mother always going before the church asking for prayers. At the time I was embarrassed, but now that I have grown in my relationship with God I see that my Mother was hungry for God. I saw God take her from glory to glory. I saw my Mother transform before my eyes as I was entering into high school. My Mother was relentless in her pursuit of God. I saw her put down cigarettes completely after smoking 3 packs a day. I saw her put down alcohol, get healthier, and become a better Mother and Grandmother.

When we make the decision to make Jesus the Lord of our life, we no longer get to pick and choose what He allows. We are made for His good purpose. Part of being a living testimony, we must be willing to die for the cause of Christ. We cannot love our lives so much that we are afraid to die (Revelation 12:11). The Holy Spirit spoke to me some time later letting me know that my Mother had to die for me to live. In the beginning I struggled to accept it. After going back over my Mother's life and her horrendous death, I could see the hand of God. Her death was God's way of getting my attention just like when Stephen was martyred for preaching the truth about Jesus. Stephen was stoned and my Mother was murdered with a hammer. Stephen stood up for righteousness and my Mother did too. Stephen's death had a lasting impact on (Saul) Paul (Acts 22). Not long after that Paul had His own encounter with God and it changed his life forever. Paul went on to become one of the greatest writers of the New Testament and Apostle of the Gospel.

As the years began to go by, I began to understand that God wanted me to continue what my Mother had started and take it to the next level and pass it on to my children (Philippians 16:1). I was very fortunate to obtain my Mother's prayer journal after her murder. After reading how she was praying for our family, it encouraged me to begin doing the same. God took what the enemy used to destroy me and turned it into a refining fire. That refining fire has been taking away any and everything that God no longer desires. I am encouraged to fan the flames of my faith so that I can persevere and not only walk in authority, but experience dominion as a result of the good work that my Mother began (2 Timothy 1:5-7). I am no longer ashamed when I suffer for righteousness sake. In fact, I laugh because I realize that God is pleased with my life. Every believer must be willing to drink the same bitter cup that Jesus drank (Matthew 20:22). It doesn't mean that we will become a martyr like my Mother. But if it's God's will, we will have the courage and strength to walk through it with peace knowing that Jesus is right there with us.

Overcoming Rejection

Paul never tells us exactly what the thorn in his flesh was that God used to keep him humble.

2 Corinthians 12:7-10 MSG states, *Because of the extravagance of those revelations, and so I wouldn't get a big head, I was given the gift of a handicap to keep me in constant touch with my limitations. Satan's angel did his best to get me down; what he in fact did was push me to my knees. No danger then of walking around high and mighty! At first I didn't think of it as a gift, and begged God to remove it. Three times I did that, and then he told me, My grace is enough; it's all you need. My strength comes into its own in your weakness. Once I heard that, I was glad to let it happen. I quit focusing on the handicap and began appreciating the gift. It was a case of Christ's strength moving in on my weakness. Now I take limitations in stride, and with good cheer, these limitations that cut me down to size—abuse, accidents, opposition, bad breaks. I just let Christ take over! And so the weaker I get, the stronger I become.*

I truly believe that God used my fear of being rejected as one of the main thorns in my flesh to keep me humble and learn how to put my complete trust in Him and Him alone. Having struggled with rejection my entire life even up until this year, I realized that as long as I looked to anyone or anything outside of God I would always fall back into my old habits. I went through several encounters that finally released me from the grips of rejection. It was imperative for me to endure the rain so I could begin to reign with Christ.

Enduring the Rain

Then Jesus said to his disciples, "If you truly want to follow me, you should at once completely reject and disown your own life. And you must be willing to share my cross and experience it as your own way, as you continually surrender to my ways.

Matthew 16:24 TPT

This scripture speaks to what we must be willing to do for the cause of Christ today.

Here are a few examples of the rain that I had to endure over the past few months that have helped me finally overcome rejection:

1. Vocal Cords-constant hoarseness that has made it difficult to speak or sing.
2. Almost bitten by a snake
3. Had the police called on me
4. Lied on.
5. Threatened to be thrown in jail.
6. Money illegally stolen from ministry.
7. Car towed from my home.
8. Room Vandalized at hotel.
9. Over 20 flights cancelled.
10. Rejected by 2 of the most important people in my life.
11. Attempts to sabotage my businesses

God sent me a warning by allowing me to see the snake to let me know that I was about to drink a bitter cup. He was letting me know that the devil was coming to tempt and test my faith like he did when Jesus started His ministry (Matthew 4). I was also tested in every area that had been hard to resist the devil in the past. I was tempted to start back gambling, hooking up with a man, falling back into depression, drinking, and overeating.

From Rejected to Redeemed

The area that was the most difficult for me was the rejection of the 2 family members, but I was able to get past those situations within 1 day of the attacks. Praise God! The old Tuwana would have struggled with it for at least a couple of months. All of these attacks were due to no wrong doing on my part. None of these encounters were provoked by me. They were meant to deter me, make me give up on God, and turn back. They were all done deliberately by the enemy to me get out of purpose.

So we must let go of every wound that has pierced us and the sin we so easily fall into. Then we will be able to run life's marathon race with passion and determination, for the path has been already marked out before us. We look away from the natural realm and we fasten our gaze onto Jesus who birthed faith within us and who leads us forward into faith's perfection. His example is this: Because his heart was focused on the joy of knowing that you would be his, he endured the agony of the cross and conquered its humiliation, and now sits exalted at the right hand of the throne of God! So consider carefully how Jesus faced such intense opposition from sinners who opposed their own souls, so that you won't become worn down and cave in under life's pressures.

Hebrews 12:1b-3 TPT

Because God warned me that these tests were coming and had on the full armor of God, I finally overcame my fear of rejection. I passed the tests because I have remained teachable. I have made it my life's focus to keep my eyes on Jesus and his example. If my Lord and Savior can be humiliated, so can I. We must be willing to die to self, endure the pain, suffer for righteousness, take up our cross and follow Jesus, and ultimately die if that's what God requires. These attacks solidified my authority through Jesus Christ.

From Rejected to Redeemed

I no longer get upset when people reject me, I recognize that when they reject me they are actually rejecting the ONE who sent me and coming against their very souls.

I pray that God will have mercy on their souls for rejecting Him. I must be about my Father's business. Everyone will not receive and it's not my job to worry about who receives me or not. They take that issue up with God. I know that all things work together for our good and for the glory of God. We must be willing to allow the world to bury us. Let the enemy think that he has left us for dead. What the enemy doesn't know is that he buried us so that the rain will process us and grow us up into who God intended for us to be. God was using all of the rain in my life to prepare me to become a lighthouse that would lead others safely to Him.

Revelation Moment

And now he has made all of this plain to us by the appearing of Christ Jesus, our Savior. He broke the power of death and illuminated the way to life and immortality through the Good News. And God chose me to be a preacher, an apostle, and a teacher of this Good News. That is why I am suffering here in prison. But I am not ashamed of it, for I know the one in whom I trust, and I am sure that he is able to guard what I have entrusted to him until the day of his return."

2 Timothy 1:9-12 NLT

From Rejected to Redeemed

I believe that no matter what limitations we may face in life, we must understand that God's grace is sufficient. He will never put more on us that we can bear. So with every trial and tribulation, we can keep our focus on Jesus, who is the author and finisher of our faith (Hebrews 12:2 KJV). Jesus was rejected so we must walk like Jesus did (1 John 2:6 KJV) and endure rejection as a test of our faithfulness to God.

The more I recognize my need for God and stay at His feet, the more he reveals to me, and the more I am empowered through the saving grace of Jesus Christ to endure the pain of rejection. Some situations that used to take me months and years to get past, now are only taking me 30 minutes to get over because I decided to live in obedience to God.

Being rejected by those most dear to my heart over the course of this past summer were simply footstools to elevate me to another level in my relationship with God. The tests that I had to endure over the years and any trials that I must endure going forward, are simply confirmations that I am walking with God and He approves of me. Listening to the voice of the enemy always leads to destruction. As long as we remain unstable allowing the enemy to dilute our minds into thinking that we can serve God and serve self too, we will never be able to operate within the authority of Jesus Christ. We must be sure of who we are and endure what the enemy throws at us and stand firm. God will give us beauty for our ashes. We must maintain a willingness to do things God's Way. The weapons will continue to form, but they cannot prosper if we stay in the will of God. In order to truly live for God, we must be willing to die to self and life as we know it. If we want to reign with Christ, we must endure the rain all for the glory of God! To God Be the Glory forever!

"Don't miss the boat of Life because you're too afraid to get wet."

-Tuwana Nicole

Chapter 24

Walk in Authority

But those who embraced him and took hold of his name were given authority to become the children of God!

John 1:12 TPT

In order to walk in authority, we must walk like Jesus did. Our reality must match God's reality for our lives. We must love without limits and live without fear. We must be obedient children who not only take on the name of Jesus, but are willing to endure the rain so we can reign with Christ. Our authenticity lies in our obedience to God. Our authority lies in our servitude to God.

Get in Position to Receive Authority

Jesus called his twelve disciples together and gave them authority to cast evil spirits and to heal every kind of disease and illness.

Matthew 10:1 NLT

We can be teaching, preaching, pastoring, prophets, who operate in the apostolic. We received all authority when we accepted Jesus as our personal Lord and Savior. God shows us our identity when we are struggling to figure it out on our own. It's up to us to believe that we are who God says we are. We can trust that if God said it, that settles it. Once we have accepted it, then we must trust Him to bring it to pass within His timing and our willingness to believe. As we endure the rain so we can reign and God sees that He can trust us then He advances us in rank and gives us more authority.

Ascend to the Throne

But you are the ones chosen by God, chosen for the high calling of priestly work, chosen to be a holy people, God's instruments to do his work and speak out for him, to tell others of the night-and-day difference he made for you—from nothing to something, from rejected to accepted.

1 Peter 2:9-10 MSG

As priests, God's royal priesthood we didn't earn this entitlement. We simply walked into the calling on each of our lives by allowing God to give us our identity in Christ. We were adopted into the Kingdom of God when we accepted Jesus's proposal to become His bride. We became Sons and Daughters, but we still need to be taught how to ascend to our thrones. We don't automatically become the King or the Queen, we must allow God to fill us with His anointing as we spend time at His feet and He trains us in His ways. The King of Kings and Lord of Lords moves us up in the ranks, the more time we spend training in His courts. The more we allow God to fill us up, the quicker we begin to walk in authority and experience dominion.

"Be good to your servant, GOD; be as good as your Word. Train me in good common sense; I'm thoroughly committed to living your way. Before I learned to answer you, I wandered all over the place, but now I'm in step with your Word. You are good, and the source of good; train me in your goodness. The godless spread lies about me, but I focus my attention on what you are saying; They're bland as a bucket of lard, while I dance to the tune of your revelation. My troubles turned out all for the best— they forced me to learn from your textbook. Truth from your mouth means more to me than striking it rich in a gold mine. With your very own hands you formed me; now breathe your wisdom over me so I can understand you. When they see me waiting, expecting your Word, those who fear you will take heart and be glad. I can see now, GOD, that your decisions are right; your testing has taught me what's true and right. Oh, love me—and right now!—hold me tight! just the way you promised. Now comfort me so I can live, really live; your revelation is the tune I dance to. Let the fast-talking tricksters be exposed as frauds; they tried to sell me a bill of goods, but I kept my mind fixed on your counsel. Let those who fear you turn to me for evidence of your wise guidance. And let me live whole and holy, soul and body, so I can always walk with my head held high."

Psalm 119:65-80 MSG

David didn't become King as soon as He received his Kingly anointing. He had to go through the process just like we do. David was anointed when he was only a boy, but he didn't actually take the throne until he was 30 years old. He didn't take over the entire kingdom until he was 37. Even though we are sealed in God when He calls us, we still must go through the process to ensure that we are ready to take our rightful place. Just like the Army, we must work our way up through the ranks.

We must be tested by the enemy and purified in the fire, buried, and go through metamorphosis. As we continue to allow this process to take place the more authority we receive.

Revelation Moment

To everyone who is victorious and continues to do my works to the very end I will give you authority over the nations to shepherd them with a royal scepter. And the rebellious will shattered as clay pots-even as I also received authority from the presence of my Father. I will give the morning star to the one who experiences victory.

Revelation 2:26-27 TPT

I am so thankful for God's continued favor over my life! I thank HIM for giving me the boldness to stand up for what's right even when others won't. I thank HIM for freeing me from the slavery of sin and the fear it brings. I thank HIM for making me a co-heir with Jesus so I can share in HIS glory now and when he comes again! What a blessing to a child of God that is ascending to the throne.

God has given me beauty for my ashes. The fire that the enemy set to destroy me, God has turned it into a refining fire to make me more into His image. Now I am a lighthouse in a world full of flashlights that walks in her God given authority!

"You can be a teaching, preaching, pastoring, prophet who walks in the apostolic."

–Tuwana Nicole

Chapter 25

Experience Dominion

Then God said, "Let us make man in our image, and after our likeness, and let them have dominion over the fish of the seas, and over the birds of the air; and over the livestock, and over all the earth, and over every creeping thing that creeps on the earth."

Genesis 1:26 MEV

Dominion is defined as sovereignty or control. The call of God is an upward call that is personal for every believer. It's all about us preparing as a king or queen to the King of Kings and Lord of Lords. When God gave us dominion over the earth in the beginning of time, it was never intended to be run the way the world is run now. We know that the devil is the god of this age and almost everything in this world comes from him.

So almost everything that we would normally consider our dominion is not what God considers dominion. We must decide if we are citizens of this world or citizens of heaven. We don't concern ourselves with building God a worldly kingdom. Our focus should be on building His heavenly Kingdom. Whatever we acquire is for the glorification of the Kingdom of God. That's why we pray, let your will be done on earth as it is in heaven.

We experience dominion when God knows that He can trust us, He will invite us to come higher. When we seek the face of God, we automatically get the hand of God.

From Rejected to Redeemed

The mountaintop is reserved for those who are willing to obey God in the valley, when He sees that we are willing to endure the rain. We must be willing to do a self-reflection daily to see where we are in our relationship with God. Now we understand that we're in this world, but we're not of this world. We must constantly check our hearts to ensure that it is in alignment with God.

God wants us to come into the fullness of who we are to Him. Life may not be a fairytale, but by resting in the fullness of God, those very dreams that we have will begin to come true without us having to compromise our relationship with God to attain them.

Greater Works

"The world is unprincipled. It's dog-eat-dog out there! The world doesn't fight fair. But we don't live or fight our battles that way—never have and never will. The tools of our trade aren't for marketing or manipulation, but they are for demolishing that entire massively corrupt culture. We use our powerful God-tools for smashing warped philosophies, tearing down barriers erected against the truth of God, fitting every loose thought and emotion and impulse into the structure of life shaped by Christ. Our tools are ready at hand for clearing the ground of every obstruction and building lives of obedience into maturity."

2 Corinthians 10:3-6 MSG

After enduring the rain to reign, being given the authority to experience dominion; if should be clear that our mandate is to shift the thought process of our culture. We experience dominion by creating a culture that longs for God and not the god of this age. We wage war through prayer and fasting, using the armor of God to keep us steady as we move forward taking territory for the Kingdom. We don't continue doing programs as usual. We speak the truth in love all while allowing the Holy Spirit to convict hearts and turn them back to Jesus. We take the worldly perspectives and show them how it leads to destruction. Then we give them Godly principles that will break generational curses and shape family legacies.

Jesus promised us that we would be able to do greater works than what He did when we walked the Earth. Modern technology like the internet has afforded us the opportunity to spread the Gospel without having to leave our home. So we have the opportunity to spread the gospel to those we may never meet in person. We have the opportunity to spread the true Kingdom of God through our testimonies.

Revelation Moment

Your kingdom is an everlasting kingdom, and your dominion endures through all generations. The Lord is trustworthy in all he promises and faithful in all he does.

Psalms 145:13 NIV

After I began moving forward at the direction of the Holy Spirit telling me to pray more, everything began to come together. I merely thought God was expanding my physical territory, but I soon began to realize that God was expanding me for my good and for His purpose by expanding the territory of His Kingdom. God was and still is shaping me into a teaching, preaching, pastoring, prophet, who operates in the apostolic. God has me traveling all over the world to pray, speak, heal, deliver, teach, and educate the body of Christ.

From Rejected to Redeemed

When we made the decision to stop wasting time and come into agreement with who God says we are, a son and daughter of the Most High God. Then and only then can we begin ascending to the throne. Once we rise to our calling we can take souls from the kingdom of darkness and transfer them into the Kingdom of God. Then we all mankind can experience dominion like God intended. By resting in paradise, we will experience what Adam and Eve experienced in the beginning. We will experience this when Jesus comes again (Revelation 22) and we have come together in unity. As the Bride of Christ, His Kings and Queens, we will have taken our right places in the kingdom and will we ready for Him to bring everything into perfect alignment. Until then we continue pressing on and enjoying the biggest treasure, our relationship with God above all else!

"Just because it looks like a loss, doesn't mean you lose."

-Tuwana Nicole

Chapter 26

Conclusion

Now all has been heard; here is the conclusion of the matter; Fear God and keep his commandments, for this is the duty of all mankind.

Ecclesiastes 12:13 NIV

Don't hurry or worry through life. Allow God to carry you through life. Everything that happens in your life is because God wants to get the glory. Whether things happened to you that were out of your control, things you brought on yourself, a test of your faith, the plan of the enemy, or from the enemy; God is a gracious and merciful God that wants you to get to know Him so we can learn how to win in life forevermore.

We know that the enemy is allowed to exist to test our faith and make us turn away from God. We must make up our minds in the beginning to never give up even when we face hard times. The weapons will continue to form against us, but we must believe that they will never prosper because of God's promises to us. Don't give up. Don't give in to the shouts of the enemy. Know that the plan of the enemy and Satan himself will ultimately self-destruct along with anyone who follows him. So don't destroy yourself because you can't just be still before God and trust that He is God!

King Solomon, the wisest man who ever lived writes in Ecclesiastes 9:11 NIV: *The race is not to the swift or the battle to the strong, nor does food come to the wise or wealth to the brilliant or favor to the learned; but time and chance happen to them all.*

From Rejected to Redeemed

There will always be a tugging on our soul for the things of the world, but if we remain in the presence of the Lord we will always make the right choice.

But the one who endures to the end will be saved.

Matthew 24:12-15 NLT

When we pursue God like we would a spouse, money, or career and are careful not to use Jesus to suit our own personal preferences, we win life. We must be careful that our acceptance of Jesus isn't simply so we will be politically correct either, yet continuing to bear the rotten fruit from the deeds of darkness. A sign of a transformed life will bear spiritual fruit that resembles Christ. Let love be our motivating factor to push forward to living a better than blessed life. We will experience a supernatural, intimate relationship with our Heavenly Father, the Creator of the Heavens and the Earth, Jesus Christ; His Son through the leading of the Holy Spirit! Go from rejected to redeemed by overcoming the plan of the enemy by enduring to the end!!

"For from Him [all things originate] and through Him [all things live and exist] and to Him are all things [directed]. To Him be glory and honor forever! Amen."

ROMANS 11:36 AMP

Stay away from all the foolish arguments of the immature, for these disputes will only generate more conflict. For a true servant of our Lord Jesus will not be argumentative, but gentle toward all and skilled in helping others see the truth, having great patience toward the immature. Then with meekness you'll be able to carefully enlighten those who argue with you so they can see God's gracious gift of repentance and be brought to the truth. This will cause them to rediscover themselves and escape from the snare of Satan who caught them in his trap so that they would carry out his purposes.

2 Timothy 2:23-26 TPT

Contact Us

If this book has helped you in any way, we would like to hear from you. Please write or fill out a contact us form with your personal testimony. If you need prayers and/or free counseling, feel free to contact us.

P.O. Box 38165
Germantown, TN 38183
OR
821 Herndon Ave Suite 141433
Orlando, FL 32814
www.betterthanblessed.com
800-736-0854

Author Bio

Tuwana Nicole earned a bachelor's degree in Business Management from Lambuth University now University of Memphis and a certification in Biblical Counseling from Light University. She is a member of the American Association of Christian Counselors. She is also a certified travel consultant and certified hydration specialist.

In spite of overwhelming personal traumatic experiences of molestation, low self-esteem, domestic violence, divorce, the murder of her mother, financial ruin, homelessness, depression, and being deathly ill; Tuwana has risen above it all to be a beacon of hope for others.

Tuwana is passionate about helping others come to know God and has committed her life to serving God. She spends her time investing in the lives of others by speaking, teaching, counseling, singing, and sharing her story.

Tuwana is the Visionary of To God Be the Glory Ministries DBA Better Than Blessed Enterprises. BTBE services include counseling, vacation planning, health & wellness, business consultation, motivational speaking, books, and apparel.
Tuwana hopes that her story will inform, inspire, and encourage all people everywhere to surrender their lives to God so they can live better than blessed!

Other Books Available

Living Better Than Blessed: A Daily Devotional to Nurture the Mind, Body, and Soul & Living Better Than Blessed Prayer Journal

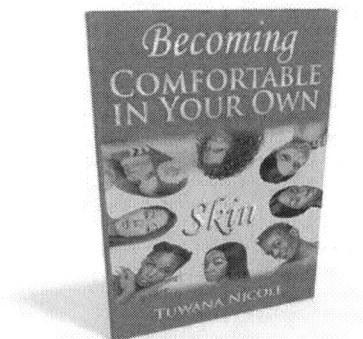

Becoming Comfortable In Your Own Skin

From Rejected to Redeemed

Made in the USA
Columbia, SC
24 September 2022